NAME: _____

DATE: _____

PHONE: _____

EMAIL: _____

"WE PRACTICE SO THAT IN THE FACE OF ADVERSITY WE CAN OVERCOME ALL ODDS!"

-MICHAEL A. JOHNSON

I would like to thank all those that have helped in the creation of this book. I am eternally grateful for the support you've given me. I'd like to thank my family for supporting me in this endeavor and my coaches for helping me become who I am today. Special thanks to my team, Andrew, Kyla, Robbie, and Ruth, you are amazing. Last but not least, thank you to Alexi Ruffell who has tirelessly worked to help me bring this project into reality. I could not have done it without you!

MJ

ISBN-13: 978-1546317005
ISBN-10: 1546317007
Copyright © 2017
Editor: Alexi Ruffell
Cover and Layout: Robbie Cromwell

The First Step
A Guide to Competitive Ballroom Dancing

Michael A. Johnson

DANCE MAJIC

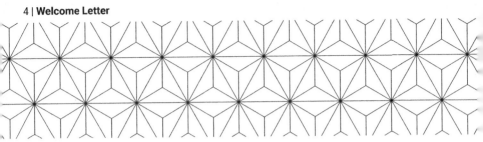

WELCOME LETTER

I imagine that if you are reading this then you have decided to take your dancing to the next level. Congratulations! This marks the beginning of an incredible journey which you will remember and enjoy for the rest of your life. Welcome aboard!

I'm excited to have the opportunity to share with you something I hold near and dear to my heart. Dance! I have been doing ballroom dance since I was five and I have been through every phase and facet of ballroom dance you can imagine. I have learned from some of the best dancers and coaches in the world, not only how to dance but also how to teach and how to coach.

I expect you to work hard. Hard work beats talent when talent doesn't work hard! I teach very systematically and anyone who has worked with me will tell you that I'm consistent. I believe that teaching core fundamentals is paramount in breeding success. Because of this I believe teaching with a firefighting method (fixing pieces and parts randomly) is detrimental to your progress as a dancer. I believe teaching fundamental skills to improve your dancing overall is a much better approach. As the the old adage goes . . . Give a man a fish and he eats for a day. Teach a man to fish and he will eat for a lifetime. It can be a tenuous process but one which will produce great results if you commit to it. I'm

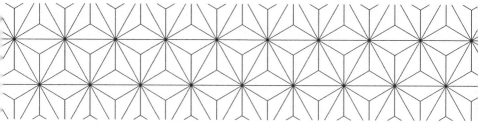

excited to guide you and share this journey with you. Through the good times and the bad I look forward to helping you grow into a fabulous dancer and an amazing person!

The following pages have been split up into sections that I believe will be helpful in finding information as you need it. I will teach you about each subject during our time together. This book will serve as a guide and a tool to help you become a high level ballroom competitor.

TABLE OF CONTENTS

WHERE ARE YOU AT?

"The first step before anybody else in the world believes it, is you have to believe it."

- Will Smith

"EVERY NEXT LEVEL
OF YOUR LIFE WILL
DEMAND A DIFFERENT
VERSION OF YOU."
-UNKNOWN

HOW SERIOUS AND HOW SOON?

In any sport, there are different levels of seriousness. Social dance was the roots of ballroom dance but like any other sport that you get involved in, there is always a much more serious level of competition.

There are many benefits that are involved with getting into ballroom dance such as the opportunity to learn important communication skills and being able to achieve a high level of physicality. While adults may enjoy ballroom in a social or pro/am setting, ballroom dance offers younger dancers opportunities to be competitive and opens up the possibilities for a future career.

The level of seriousness can be defined by the number of private lessons you and your partner have each week, the amount of practice, the number of competitions you do in your local area, and how often you travel to compete. In the early stages , doing local competitions is good.As you become more serious, you will need to be seen by more judges and gain more experience.

Seriousness in practice comes as you commit to practice more. You can refer to "Practicing" for more information.

As you continue to take private coaching, it is best to start taking lessons from professionals who visit your local area. As you continue down that path, you might consider traveling with your partner to take lessons from professionals outside your area.

Your level of commitment will determine the quality of your costuming and whether you have your outfit custom made or rented. The quality of costume and appearance reflects your seriousness. Refer to the section on costuming in "Competitions" for more specific details.

As you determine your seriousness, you can then chart your best course of action consulting with your partner and coach.

LEVELS

If you want to be successful in any sport, there are going to be necessary steps involved for success. In this section, there will be three levels presented. The first level refers to the syllabus category and first time ballroom dancers. The second level covers dancers in their first or second year of open, and the third level presented is for those who are versed ballroom dancers and are very committed to the sport. We will discuss what you generally need to

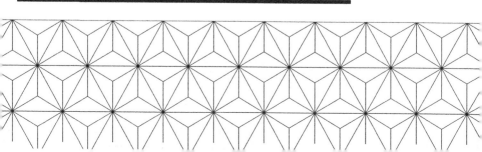

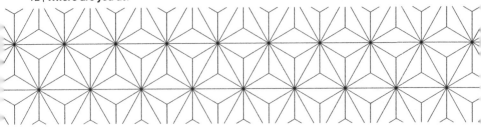

know for each level and what to prepare for when you become serious about competitive ballroom dance.

First Level

For beginning dancers, the minimum amount of lessons you should have a week is one lesson. Group classes are a good option at this stage because it is less expensive and it gives you broader experience with other kids that are learning the same things as you. You will learn, progress, and your dancing will improve.

IT IS IMPORTANT THAT YOU LEARN THE SYLLABUS DANCES, FIGURES, AND TECHNIQUE BEFORE YOU MOVE UP INTO OPEN.

As with any sport, you need to practice what you are learning. Depending on how involved you are and how many lessons you have a week, you can adjust how often you practice. I recommend starting with two practices a week when you are just taking a group class.

When you are new to ballroom, you can compete in the local competitions. These, of course, are cheaper than out of state competitions because you do not have the added costs of travel or hotels.

Second Level

Once you have been in syllabus for a while and have learned the necessary fundamentals, you may be ready to move up in the ranks and become an open level dancer. Ideally you would have competed bronze, silver, and gold syllabus. Please see *Syllabus Is Important* in

"Practicing." At this level you should have a minimum of two lessons a week and practice two hours every day.

We want to emphasize that it is important that you learn the syllabus dances, figures, and technique before you move up into open. Not going into open too soon allows you to gain a very strong foundation in ballroom and it will make it so later down the road, you do not have to go back and learn the basic figures. Again, you can achieve this knowledge by taking private lessons and participating in group classes. Group classes do not offer one on one interactions, they allow you to learn general skills and core fundamentals.

Some of the differences between competing in syllabus and open are the costumes you are allowed to wear and the difficulty of choreography you can dance. For a dancer at this level, it is ideal to have two privates a week with a coach. When you move into open, you need to consider getting lessons for each style that you dance. If you are doing Latin and Standard you need to have a lesson in each style each week.

At this state you will have many different routines and since the open category is more competitive than syllabus, more practice time will be necessary for you to fully apply what you are learning. Making a commitment to dance and keeping that commitment for at least two hours everyday, 6 days a week, is essential for success.

Costumes at this stage are very important. You will no longer be wearing the syllabus attire and first impressions are a big deal! When you walk out onto the floor, having a good looking costume makes a big difference. There are lots of options for getting ballroom competition attire. You can rent, you can buy from someone locally or you can buy something online. Be cautious when buying a costume from the internet because what is pictured is not always what you get, but you can always alter the costume. The other option is to custom make a costume. This option is more expensive and if you are just starting in open, then making a costume might be something you do after more experience has been gained.

Third Level

Now that you have been in competitive ballroom dance for some time, it is important that you have lessons every week with your core coach for each of the styles that you are participating in with additional lessons from professionals. Having lessons with professionals allows them to get to know you and you to gain valuable information. Talk with your coach about the appropriate amount of lessons with professionals for your partnership. At this stage, it is important to

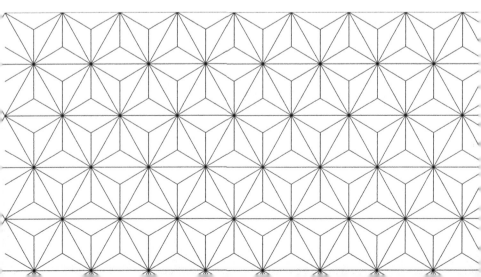

attend as many out of state competitions as you are able. You should make it a priority to practice two to four hours a day, six days a week and you should focus on more competitive goals.

Local competitions are now good for floor time or for you to have your dancing videoed so you can analyze it later in practice. Out of state competitions should be attended as often as possible because it offers exposure to important judges and competitors.

Costumes should look professional and be good quality. Ballroom is a subjective sport and having a good quality costume is key. At this stage having a custom costume made becomes more imperative.

"EVERYONE WANTS TO BE SUCCESSFUL UNTIL THEY SEE WHAT IT ACTUALLY TAKES."
-UNKNOWN

CREATING A TEAM

"A coach is someone who always makes you do what you don't want to do so you can be who you've always wanted to be."

-Unknown

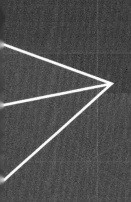

> "ALONE WE CAN DO SO LITTLE; TOGETHER WE CAN DO SO MUCH."
> —HELEN KELLER

HAVING A TEAM

Having a good team is a vital component to achieving a high level of skill and knowledge. As with anything, if we want to attain high levels of proficiency, we must have a strong supporting cast to help us attain our goals. In the beginning, this supporting cast should start small and as you progress you can add members to your team as you and your main coach see fit.

Your initial team will be simple and straight-forward. It will consist of you, your parents, your partner and their parents, and your main coach. In the early years of your dancing (under the age of 17) it is important that your parents meet often as they are an integral part of your success. Coordination between parents of the partnership can be challenging but with the help and direction from your main coach it will be much easier.

As you progress, your main coach will have multiple responsibilities. It is the job of the main coach to help you establish a plan for your progress through your season. Your main coach will initially take care of all facets of your partnership including teaching you new core skills,teaching you how to practice, working on performance and "the IT factor", planning a competition schedule, planning outside coaching, and planning costuming.

In the early years of a partnership and of your dancing, having a main coach is essential to teach you and guide you. As your needs grow more advanced it will be important to carefully add members to your team. In later stages of an advanced partnership, your main coach will help you work through information you receive from other teachers you are privileged to take lessons from along the way. In many instances, working on new knowledge gained from visiting coaches with your main coach will help you solidify what you have learned.

A typical professional partnership will have an extensive team including their main coach, a number of teachers in their inner circle of advisors and then multiple teachers that help support the overall goal of progression in their dancing. Also included on their team are costume makers, shoe companies and hair designers.

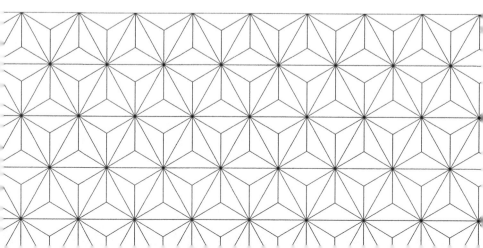

Below is the retirement speech from retired Professional Smooth Champions, Slawek and Marzena Sochacki. It is a wonderful example of how a team, in the professional ranks, was put together.

We feel so honored and proud that we have been able to learn and compete in this amazing style while sharing the floor with incredible dancers. Dancers that we respect, dancers who respect each other while still competing fiercely with one another. Most amazing is that we all enjoy special friendships. We want to thank all of them for making these years so memorable.

We want to send special thanks to our Loving Families and our son Lukasz, who have travelled to over 70 competitions, plus many shows and coaching trips. Without their sacrifices, love and support our success wouldn't be possible. For the last 5 years they were living our lives—taking time away from theirs—so we could practice and compete. We will be forever grateful for every moment that we spent together, as a family, traveling around the world. Those memories are priceless and will stay in our hearts forever.

Thank you to our amazing sponsors:
- Ballroom Playlist for inspiring music
- Dancelife USA for shoes
- Park West Photography for many amazing memories
- The Winning Look for our beautiful tans
- Boyko and Company for stunning hair and makeup
- Dr. Sten Kervin for keeping our bodies healthy and in shape
- And LeNique for their truly amazing vision and their creations that will be never forgotten.

There are people that have changed our lives for the better and we can't forget about them:
- Alan Dixon and Stuart Cole who gave us a new start in our life in the United States at Vivo Dancesport Center
- John DePalma for teaching us the business values that have helped us and changed our lives forever
- Pat West and the Londance staff for the most amazing work experience and for so much help with our son during our first year of competing in American Smooth
- our amazing Students who have been willing to adjust their schedules to ours.
- and our fans that were making us to dance to our maximum.

There are 2 ladies that could not be forgotten. We were never sponsored by them but definitely their help could not be unnoticed

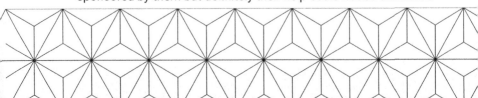

• Mary Tweedle for so many amazing pictures
• And Cassandra Valeria for all the help with shoes
We would like to thank all of the coaches that have shared their knowledge and passion with us over the last 17 years. Especially: Irena Stachura, Mariusz Smolenski , Graham Oswick, Stephen Hannah, Nadia Eftedal , Michael and Vicky Baar, Julie Fryer, Rufus Dustin, Stuart Cole, Linda Dean, Mariusz 'Mario' Olszewski , Brian and Sue Puttock, Sharon Savoy , Michael Mead, Max Winkelhuis, Tony Meredith and Richard Porter (not only for 9 years of training but as well for giving us opportunity to come to the U.S.).

Our special thanks to Nick Kosovich and Kosovich Lena for not only their knowledge, passion and friendship, but for being the most amazing sponsors a couple could ever have.

Our deepest thanks goes to our Amazing Dream Team. This is the Team that had the biggest impact on our success. Every sportsman and dancer should find a team of coaches that not only provides knowledge, but shares their passion, who you can trust, who believes in you, and who, most importantly, allow you to grow as individuals. Our Team has been by our side from 2009 and a couple of them were with us from the beginning of our journey in the United States back in 2002. They have inspired us in so many ways and they have become more than teachers. They became our friends. We would like to take this opportunity and acknowledge the five members of our "Dream Team:"
• Olga Foraponova Wright
• David Hamilton
• Wolfgang Opitz
• Heather Smith
• And special thanks to "Head Hunter" Toni Redpath . If not for her, we would have never discovered our love and passion for American Smooth. She was the one that saw something in us. By asking us for only a 1-year adventure, she became the one who opened so many new doors for us. We will never be able to thank her enough for the opportunity that she gave us.

We can only hope that we have inspired, touched and helped to move American Smooth to a higher level. We want to wish continued success in this process to all our fellow competitors.
Sincerely,
4-time United States and 4-time World reigning and undefeated Open American Smooth Champions
Marzena Stachura and Slawek Sochacki

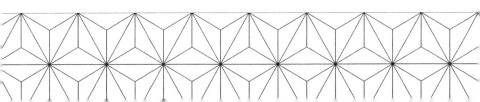

WHAT TO EXPECT FROM A MAIN COACH

Choosing a coach is a very crucial step when going into competitive ballroom dance. Your core coach has many responsibilities when it comes to your dancing.They will take great pride in helping you to attain your goals and aspirations in dance. They will be your teacher, coach, and guide on this wonderful journey. A main coach is there to help you create your plan of action in all of the different facets of your dancing, from planning your practice time to planning costumes.

You should expect your coach to teach you the core fundamental skills that will help you improve from the inside out. They should push you beyond your perceived limits, help you to chase your dreams, help you get through the hard times, and celebrate with you during the great times.

YOU SHOULD EXPECT YOUR COACH TO TEACH YOU THE CORE FUNDAMENTAL SKILLS THAT WILL HELP YOU IMPROVE FROM THE INSIDE OUT.

It is important that you become an outstanding, contributing member of society; therefore helping you to become the best person you can be is of utmost importance in your dance progression. Few will make it into the professional ranks of the dance world. So for those not heading that direction, dance will help you become a great person with fabulous work ethics that you can take with you into whatever profession you eventually choose. However, for those that are considering a professional career in dance, your core coach should be able to help you take the necessary steps to reach that goal.

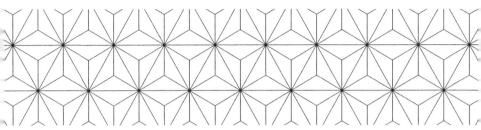

There are many things to learn along the way. Your coach should be excited to help you get educated about the best ways to attain your goals.

Inevitably partnerships will have challenges. Your core coach should help you work through those challenges and help you to learn better ways to communicate so you can create a long lasting partnership that can withstand the bumps in the road.

Choosing a coach and having them become involved can take time so be patient and dedicated to your coach. By being loyal, you will create a team that leads you to success.

SUCCESSFUL PARTNERSHIPS

Creating a long lasting partnership should be your highest priority. The most successful partnerships in the industry have been together for years and have been able to continue their progression more efficiently. Remember that each time you split up with your partner you have to start over with new choreography and gain a new skill set for that specific partnership. Long lasting partnerships can be tough to obtain in your journey to reach your goals. Do not give up on the partnership the minute there are problems because things will go wrong. It is easy to appreciate your partner on the days that things are going well but how do you get through the days that don't go so well? Here are some tips on maintaining a successful partnership:

- Communication is key! If you don't say it, your partner doesn't know it. Nor are they responsible to read your mind.
- Get to know your partner as you would a friend. When your partner feels comfortable around you, they will confide in you.
- It is imperative that you understand that you and your partner are individual and different people. You accomplish your goals differently and you must work together to overcome these differences.
- Focus on what YOU need to improve on and then focus on the solution to the problem, not on whose fault it is.
- On the days that are going badly it is beneficial to change your focus. Focus on you, watch videos, take a break, eat something!
- Remember that when things are going badly it is between you, your partner, and your coach. Keep your peers out of it and bring your coach into it.
- Belief will carry the partnership. Believe in your partner and treat them like they are the best at all times

Make a list of all of the amazing things about your partner below. . . This is a great tool when you need a reminder of how good your partner is. Also included in the workbook section are many ideas on how to continue to enhance your partnership.

Amazing Things About My Partner:

1. _____
2. _____
3. _____
4. _____
5. _____
6. _____
7. _____
8. _____
9. _____
10. _____

"DON'T LOOK FOR A PARTNER WHO IS EYE CANDY. LOOK FOR A PARTNER WHO IS SOUL FOOD."

-KAREN SALMANSHOHN

AUDITION PROCESS

Each coach runs auditions slightly differently. You may need to schedule a full lesson for the try out or you may have a miniature private lesson with your coach and your potential partner. You will learn one or two simple pieces of choreography to see the level you are at and the level of the person you are auditioning with. This will help you determine if your levels coincide with one another. The coach will then offer advice on what they see in this potential partnership. After hearing from the coach, you need to speak with the other partner and their parents and talk about the logistics. It is important to make sure that you choose a person that is right for you, your lifestyle, and your dance goals. Before asking these questions, know your expectations and your goals. Your thoughts and expectations need to be clear between you and your potential

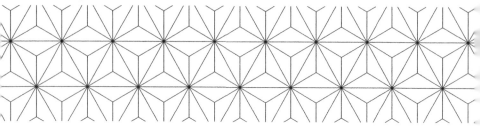

partner. This is where you lay the groundwork for effective communication in the future.

Make sure that you have someone video your tryout choreography at the end. Take notes about the logistics after the tryout is over. Later this will help you review and have something to refer back to when you are making a decision.

Here is a list of questions that you should talk about:

- What are your goals?
- How many hours are you willing to practice each day and each week?
- What are you able to put into dance financially?
- How many competitions are you willing to attend and if so, what competitions would you like to do?
- Who do you want your core coach to be?
- Are there other coaches you would like on the team?
- How many lessons a week would you like to take?
- Do you want to take lessons with professionals that are brought in from other states?
- What does a good practice look like to you vs. a bad practice ?
- What styles of dance do you want to do/what style do you want to focus on?
- What is your daily and weekly schedule look like currently?

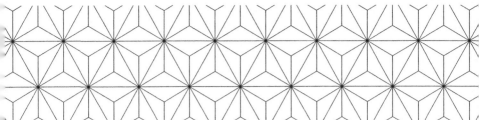

After asking questions, you can then determine if proceeding with the partnership would be a good decision. There is no limit to the amount of auditions you can have, but make sure to be reasonable when selecting people to tryout with. When you are evaluating partnership options, make a list of your top picks and inform the first person on your list that you want to dance with them. Keep in mind that they may have already selected someone else to be their partner or their priorities may not align with yours. In that case, you will need to look at your next best option and proceed from there. After you have made a decision, contact all of the other people you auditioned with and inform them you have made a decision.

What if you cannot find a partner? There are still options! One option is to participate in Pro-Am. Pro- Am is where an amateur dances with a professional. In Pro-am, you will be competing against other people in your age category and skill level. You can compete in Bronze, Silver, Gold and Open. Pro-Am allows you to progress and learn and is a great opportunity for you if you cannot find a partner.

You also want to make sure you take group classes. By doing this, you are still progressing and when a partnership opportunity arises, your skills can be at the level you need them to be at to get a partner. Even though group classes are not always a one on one interaction, you will still gain a technical knowledge and also learn from the mistakes and challenges of your peers. Talk to your coach and your studio about what group classes are available.

GOALS

"You must decide exactly what it is you want in life; no one can do this for you."

-Brian Tracy

"YOU'RE EITHER IN OR YOU'RE OUT. THERE IS NO SUCH THING AS LIFE IN BETWEEN."

-PAT RILEY

COMMITMENT

Now that you have picked a partner, the logistics need to be decided and agreed upon. You can use the *Create your Partnership* page in the workbook to establish what you want to commit to as a partnership in order to reach your goals. The first commitment is to dance together for a season, which is normally one year. In addition, decide who is going to make up your team, how many lessons you are going to have each week, the amount of time you are going to practice, and the competitions you will compete at. The logistics will help you reach your goals and prevent misunderstandings later on as the partnership progresses.

BASIC GOAL SETTING

Goal setting is a way of telling yourself what you are going to accomplish by creating a target to aim for. We have all had success and failures setting goals in our life. The trick is using your goal to keep you on course.

Set goals that are reasonable and lofty. If you limit yourself then there is no telling if you could have ever reached something more. The way you describe your goals can change your mindset and outlook. When you describe your goals as realistic rather than reasonable you may limit your growth. When you describe your goals as reasonable and lofty, you will be able to push yourself enough to be able to succeed.

3 Simple Steps to Attaining a Goal:
1. Decide what you want!
2. What is the time frame?
3. Why do you want it?

Decide what you want.
Although this step seems simple, it is probably the most failed step of all time. Everybody thinks they know what they want, but in many cases they don't take the time to figure out what they want specifically. This can be a daunting task and for some reason many people don't actually take the time to write down their goals on paper. I have found that the things I have written down have more often come to life than goals that I have had in my head. A very effective practice is to brainstorm your goals every so often and then rank the things that are most important to you. In the specific case of dance, you will find that there are end goals and then there are other smaller goals along the way in order to achieve that end goal. Regardless if you're making a long term goal or a short term goal, your process remains the same. You must know what you want specifically, you must write it down, and you must put it everywhere so you can see it and think about it on a consistent basis. There is a place for you to do this in the workbook.

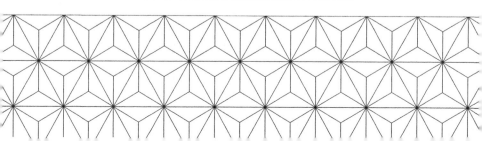

What is your time frame?

This step of the process is seemingly the easiest. However, while at first you may have an idea of how soon you should be able to achieve your goals it is important to figure out if your goal is impossible, easy, reasonable, or lofty. Limiting the human potential can often destroy our spirit. Some of the most amazing things humans have created have come from people who pushed beyond what was impossible and shot for things that were lofty. When it comes to setting time frames for goals, using the word reasonable is often a good practice. While I believe goals should be lofty and we shouldn't limit ourselves, we are all bound by time. Because of this we must find reasonable amounts of time to accomplish the things we set out to do that are lofty. For example if you set a goal to lose 20 pounds and your time frame is 3 days this is probably not reasonable without cutting off a limb or 3. Losing 20 pounds over a longer period of time, no matter how lofty it seems, is probably reasonable as long as the time frame permits. Please understand I believe we as a human race can achieve things beyond our imagination and my hope is that you will set goals that challenge you and push you past your comfort zone. A simple way to work this out is using a goal timeline. Place your goal on the far right of the timeline and determine how many weeks, months, or years you will initially allot to attain that goal. Decide what mini goals will indicate you are still heading towards your target and put them on your timeline.

There are different types of goals:

- Daily: This is your daily practice schedule.
- Weekly: This is your weekly practice schedule
- Monthly/Competition: The things you want to accomplish at your next comp

An example of a timeline can be found below.

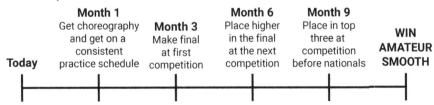

Why do you want it?

This is the most important part of setting a goal. Once you have decided specifically what you want and what time frame you want it in, now you need fuel for the engine. You must decide WHY! While many people are willing to set goals most of those goals go by the wayside because they don't have a sufficient amount of purpose behind them to drive them to completion. Think back to goals you haven't accomplished and I bet there is a lack of "why's" that supported that goal. On the other hand think about a goal that you have accomplished and think about all of the reasons why that goal had to be attained. You must have a massive amount of "why's" if you are to attain your lofty goals. One of the easiest ways to accomplish this is a simple brainstorming session. Get out your favorite playlist, put on your headphones, and jam out. Write down every possible reason why you must achieve your goal and when you think you've written enough, take a break and come back to it and write some more "why's". There is a place in the attached workbook to do this.

"RESULTS ARE INEVITABLE. . . . IF YOU DON'T HAVE YOUR OWN PLAN, SOMEONE ELSE IS GOING TO MAKE YOU FIT INTO THEIR PLAN."

-ANTHONY ROBBINS

WHAT YOU NEED

"Everything you're going through is preparing you for what you asked for."

-Unknown

"BY FAILING TO PREPARE YOU ARE PREPARING TO FAIL."
-BENJAMIN FRANKLIN

THINGS THAT YOU NEED

Below is a list of things that you need to bring with you to your practices and lessons. A list of things you need for competitions can be found in the "Competitions." Each of these items will be necessary for efficiency, hygiene, and/or personal needs.

- The dance journal included at the end of this book.
- Dance bag
- Appropriate shoes: standard pumps, latin sandals, smooth shoes, practice shoes
- Practice and lesson attire (see Dress the Part after this section for more information)
- Hair accessories
- Towel
- Deodorant
- Water bottle

- Snacks
- Music if you need it
- Band-Aids
- Vaseline for patent leathers

DRESS THE PART

Ballroom is a subjective sport thus how you present yourself is imperative. Discover your look as a partnership and execute this through your costumes, hair, and makeup. Dressing the part is just as important when you take lessons and practice on your own. You spend extreme amounts of time and money on your dancing, so it is important that you put the time and effort into the way you look on and off the floor. Look professional and show your commitment by the way you dress.

Expected attire for lessons and practice:
Boys
- Shirt and Tie or a tight fitting turtleneck under armor type shirt for Ballroom and Smooth; dress slacks or latin pants
- Latin pants and a fitted shirt for Latin

Girls
- Latin skirts and fitted shirt, blouse, or leotard.
- Standard skirt and fitted shirt, blouse, or leotard.
- For practice you may wear shorts or leggings.

When you look good, you feel good. If you like what you are wearing, what your hair looks like, and what your makeup looks like then you are most likely going to dance better. Be aware to what puts you in the best state at the studio.

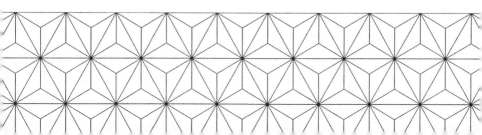

TAKING LESSONS

"The separation of talent and skill is one of the greatest misunderstood concepts, talent you have naturally, skill is only developed by hours and hours and hours of beating on your craft."

- Will Smith

"IF YOU ARE NOT WILLING TO LEARN, NO ONE CAN HELP YOU. IF YOU ARE DETERMINED TO LEARN, NO ONE CAN STOP YOU."

-UNKNOWN

TAKING LESSONS

Taking lessons is a crucial part to your development as a dancer. To improve at a quicker rate it is recommended that you take at least one lesson per week on each style that you are competing in. Lesson time with your core coach is a time for you to receive personal instruction for you to incorporate into your daily practice schedule. Lesson time is also a time to continue on a path that is specific to your improvement. When you begin to expand your team and take lessons with outside influences, consistent lessons with your core coach will help you incorporate the information you learn.

GETTING CHOREOGRAPHY

Getting choreography is the next step in your process as a partnership. You should plan on taking one or two lessons per dance in order to get your routines. Since you know what your first competition will be based on your commitment page (in the workbook), you can plan to get your choreography done in time and danceable. Once you have your routines up to speed, the next step is to improve your core dancing.

TAKING NOTES

After your lessons each week take a moment to write down the things that you learned while they are fresh on your mind. Taking notes is a way for you to sort out your thoughts and write down the key points. Your notes don't have to be detailed; you can simply make a bullet point list. Taking 5- 10 minutes of notes creates information that you can refer to at anytime, especially when putting together your practice schedule (see "Practicing" to find how to set up your practice schedule).

OUTSIDE INFLUENCES

There will be a point in your dancing when you will be ready to begin taking lessons from visiting professionals. Periodically, teachers are brought in from other states to teach. In these instances it can be very cost effective to get lessons because you don't have the added expense of traveling. Getting lessons from these visiting professionals can give you a fresh perspective to help you and your coach continue your progress. You may even receive old information from a teacher that turns a light bulb on for you because they say it in a new way.

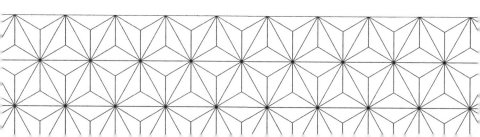

Taking lessons from visiting professionals can also help improve your connections in the ballroom industry. In turn, that helps you on the path to be better recognized when you step on to the competitive floor. As you begin to consider adding these types of lessons, it will be vital that you share your knowledge with your main coach so they can help you sort out the information for better understanding. They can then hold you accountable for applying what you have learned.

OVER THE COURSE OF TIME AND AS YOU BECOME MORE ADVANCED, YOU WILL START TO DEVELOP AN INNER CIRCLE OF TEACHERS TO ADD TO YOUR TEAM.

Over the course of time and as you become more advanced, you will start to develop an inner circle of teachers to add to your team. This team will be vital to your success.

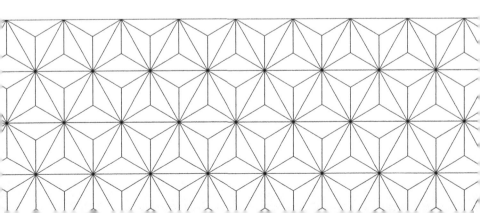

"ONE'S DESTINATION
IS NEVER A PLACE,
BUT A NEW WAY OF
SEEING THINGS."
-HENRY MILLER

TRAVELING TO GET LESSONS

As you become more advanced, the need to travel to get lessons becomes more important. There are teachers in the industry that no longer travel and others that their lesson fees are so high that it makes more sense to go to them then it does to try to bring them to you. These teachers are usually in high demand and are extremely worth traveling for to have the opportunity to work with them. It is best to plan this out carefully with your main coach to ensure you are ready for this level of instruction.

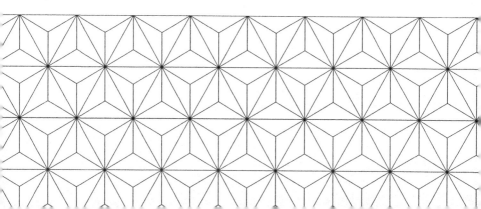

PRACTICING

"If you really look closely, most overnight successes took a long time."

-Steve Jobs

"IT'S NOT WHAT WE DO
ONCE IN AWHILE THAT
SHAPES OUR LIVES.
IT'S WHAT WE DO
CONSISTENTLY."
-ANTHONY ROBBINS

THE KEYS TO PRACTICING

To find success in dance you will need to become more consistent in your practice time. While practicing everyday creates consistency, it is even better is if you practice each day with a specific plan. You will accomplish more when you follow a plan and are productive in the amount of time that you have to practice. As you strive to reach your goals there are some simple things that will help you during your practice time.

- Schedule your practices with your partner (See figure 1 on how to set up your practice schedule)
- Plan where and what time you are going to practice each day
- Set up an outline for what you are going to do in your practice
- Split up your time appropriately between styles (if applicable)

- Stick to the plan
- Arrive to practice on time
- Wear attire that you feel good in and is appropriate for the style you are dancing
- Record yourself on a regular basis so you have a visual representation of what you are putting on the competition floor
- Practice what you did in your lesson and apply the concept to as many sections of your dancing that you can

In dealing with hundreds of students over the years I have developed a system for practicing that has proven to be successful. I have discovered that people get bored when they have to practice the same thing everyday. In order to account for this I created a practice schedule that is flexible and allows you to create a schedule that can best work for you and your partner's style of practice and your personalities. The practice schedule follows the methodology of sports teams and other types of dancing by running drills and allotting blocks of time for different areas of your dancing. It is also beneficial to plan a week rather than just planning a single day. Planning your week is beneficial in multiple ways. First, it helps you and your partner plan for the times each day that you will practice and make sure you're both on the same page for the week (which cuts down on miscommunication in the partnership). Second, it allows you the ability to maintain your time schedule during each day of practice without feeling like you're giving up on a subject before you have it "perfect". Third when you build a whole week at a time you can see a larger picture of your overall practice time. This allows you to make sure you have created a balanced schedule where you aren't over practicing one dance and giving no attention to another dance. As I have implemented this schedule with

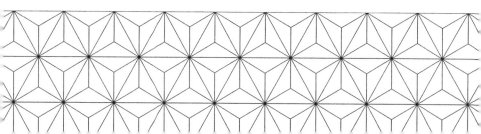

hundreds of dancers I have found that people get stuck practicing one thing with the idea that they can "get it" during that block of time and then not have to come back to it. This is a mistake of disastrous proportions. In all forms of dance and athletics it is easily seen that repetition is the mother of skill. Perfect practice does not make perfect because perfection does not exist. Looking at the big picture of the weekly schedule will help you keep on track and implement a consistent application of repetition. I have been asked what happens if more time for a particular subject was not included in the weekly schedule? With the practice schedule format I have created, the daily schedule can easily be adapted by moving other practice blocks around or removing them from your week and putting them in when you create the next weeks practice schedule.

Below I have listed and described the elements of the practice schedule. I have found that the first few weeks that you implement it, you will likely have some growing pains. Please remember that you are the master of your schedule and you can adjust it in ways that best suit you and your partner. We highly encourage you to be strict to the time you have allotted each block so that you can develop good and new habits of practicing. As you create and use your practice schedules, you will find that the amount that you can get done will increase your productivity far beyond the old worn out methods of practice taught in the past.

SETTING UP YOUR PRACTICE SCHEDULE-
Set up your schedule using these five elements:
- **Time:** The amount of time that you are willing to spend on each dance, focus, type, and style.
- **Dance:** The specific dance or dances you are rehearsing during that time.
- **Focus:** The concept you are focusing on in the specific dance or dances you are rehearsing.

  This is the meat of the practice schedule! This is the block where you place main subjects. You can focus on the things that you have learned in your lesson time as well as the technique. Use your lesson notes with you bullet point list to fill in this block. In addition review old notes and place those things in the **Focus** time block to gain repetition.
- **Type:** This element is divided into three different types of practice.

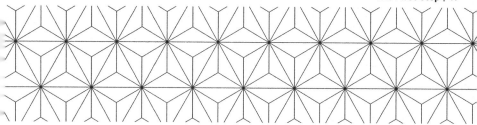

Impractical: This is when you work on the technique and the fundamentals of your dancing without dancing it in your routine. This is a great place to do exercises or drills you receive from your coaches. All great athletes have many exercises and drills that they do daily.

Semi-practical: This is when you focus on a specific concept and apply it to certain sections of your routine slowly.

Practical: This is when you apply what you have been working onin a full-out manner. This is when you utilize music.

These three types are a format of learning that has been done for years in ballet. The impractical type is similar to what ballet dancers do at the barre. Each day, they do exercises that improve their muscle memory and strength. The semi-practical type is similar to what ballet dancers when they do center work and across the floor. They do combinations and work on a specific concept and applying it. The practical type is similar to working on choreography. They have taken what they have practiced at the barre and center and applied it in full, with music.

- **Success:** In this column decide if you have completed it or it needs to be added to a different day to repeat again. You can use any method of writing it down. We like the words completed or repeat.

Here are three examples on ways you can create a practice schedule. Remember that you can adjust and remove blocks as needed.

Example 1:

Time	What	Focus	Type	Success
15 min	Rumba	Walks	Impractical	completed
15 min	Samba	Timing	Semi-Practical	completed
15 min	Foxtrot	Competition Video	Practical	repeat
15 min	Standard Round	Physical Energy	Practical	completed

Example 2:

Time	What	Focus	Type	Success
20 min	Smooth Tango	Volume	Semi-Practical	completed
20 min	Smooth Waltz	Expansion/Contraction	Semi-Practical	completed
20 min	Smooth Round	Performance	Practical	repeat

Example 3:

Time	What	Focus	Type	Success
15 min	Cha cha	Shading/first 30 sec.	Semi-Practical	completed
15 min	Samba	Timing/second 30 sec.	Semi-Practical	completed
15 min	Standard Walks	Foot Pressure	Impractical	repeat
15 min	Viennese Waltz	Natural turns	Practical	completed

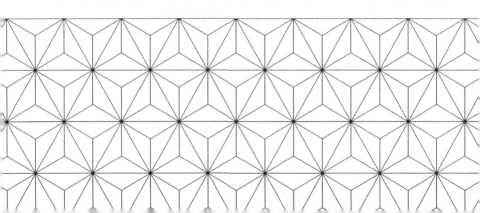

PRACTICE ROOM ETIQUETTE

The energy of many working hard and striving to improve is paramount in our speedy progression as dancers. A certain code of conduct and etiquette must be upheld in any studio that you practice at. Studios will differ in what they expect so take time to learn the proper etiquette. Below are a list of things that will most likely be applicable to any studio you go to.

- The lesson(s) being taught at any given time MUST be the priority in the room.
- If the coach wants the music, they get the music.
- If a lesson is happening in a certain part of the room move without being asked.
- Although floor-craft is a necessary skill, the couple(s) having a lesson are not required to navigate around you during their lesson. Instead please move if you recognize they are coming or need the space.
- Leave your bags where they are expected to be (dressing room, outside the ballroom floor, etc.)
- If you think you might smell bad or you are worried that you smell bad please take care of it. Deodorant, new shirt, perfume, cologne, body spray, whatever is necessary to be courteous to your partner, those practicing, and those having lessons around you.
- Do not throw your stuff all over the floor, the practice room is not your bedroom.
- Take everything you brought with you when you leave. Wrappers, Band-Aids, clothes, shoes, water bottles etc.
- Come ready to work hard and practice hard!

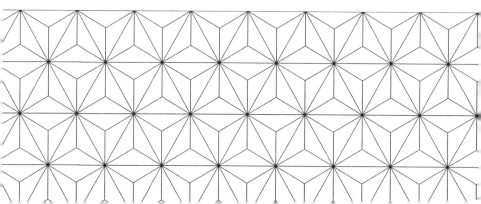

SYLLABUS IS IMPORTANT

In all forms of dancing the best dancers in the world are working on their fundamentals (syllabus) on a regular basis. In hindsight they wish they had focused on syllabus more when they were just getting into dance. In the jazz world they not only work on their individual dancing in private lessons and on their own, but in classes. This is expected, not a recommendation in other forms of dancing and should be in ballroom as well. Everyone should be taking a syllabus class and

IT IS IMPORTANT TO LEARN SYLLABUS SEQUENCES AND FIGURES IN ORDER TO PRACTICE CONTINUITY OF BASIC AND ADVANCED TECHNICAL SKILLS TO GAIN MASTERY OVER YOUR BODY.

working on syllabus routines and technical skill. Be open-minded to this idea in order to become a better dancer and prepare for long-term success. Sometimes as a high level dancer you must put aside your pride and take syllabus classes with lower level dancers. This is allows you to focus on basic technique that you might not have otherwise had the time to work on in your personal practice.

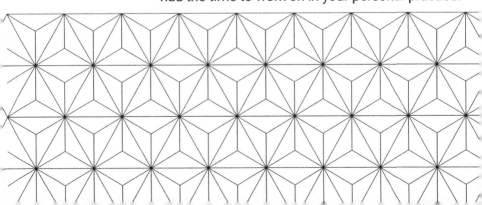

"AS A KID GROWING UP, I NEVER SKIPPED STEPS. I ALWAYS WORKED ON FUNDAMENTALS BECAUSE I KNOW ATHLETICISM IS FLEETING."

-KOBE BRYANT

How does syllabus work?

Syllabus is split up into 3 different levels that build upon each other.

- **Bronze:** The basics that give you specific components to improve your motor skills.

- **Silver:** The next level once you have gained the skills necessary from bronze. More figures are added at this level in addition to more technical elements.

- **Gold:** A more advanced level of figures and technical skill. In this stage a strong base of bronze and silver will be necessary. At this level, technique is now an imperative part of executing new figures as well as old in order to properly prepare you both physically and mentally to take the next step towards becoming an open level dancer.

It is important to learn syllabus sequences and figures in order to practice continuity of basic and advanced technical skills to gain mastery over your body.

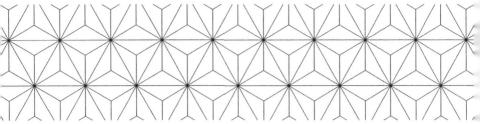

ROUNDS

Rounds are done to prepare for competitions. A round consists of running all of your dances back-to-back just as you would in the semi-final and final of a competition. You should do rounds on a regular basis and more rigorously leading up to competitions. Create a habit of doing rounds in order to build strength and endurance. Rounds run by a coach will typically be provided around major competitions; rounds with a coach are a great way to push hard with other competitors and practice your floor craft.

Pushing hard with your partner is beneficial. It can also be frustrating at times. In order to continue progressing, talk about the round with your partner. Plan to talk about three things that went well and at least one thing that you can improve on when you are done. In your next round focus on the things that you need to work on.

PRACTICING ON YOUR OWN

Practicing with your partner is essential and required for success, however practicing by yourself is very important and most dancers don't do enough of it. Many professionals in the industry practice on their own because they often spend their days teaching. This allows them to continue to improve even though they might not get all of the partnering time they would like.

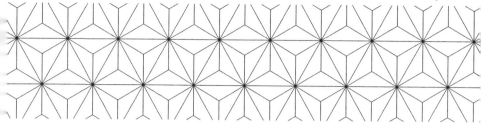

As with anything, personal improvement is always a priority. Practicing on your own allows you to review routines and technique and go at a pace that is perfect for you. Not only does the partnership have to be good and improving, you also need to be the best individual dancer on the floor. When it comes to ballroom dancing, people often focus on the partnership getting better. When you practice by yourself and improve your dancing on a personal level, you are adding to the partnership, not subtracting. Continue to improve individually and hold yourself to a higher standard. If you do not practice by yourself, you become a leach to the partnership and you have to spend more time on the execution of the figures. This often leads to arguments and discontent between you and your partner and can create a very negative experience. Without a doubt, every champion in the professional ballroom world has become that champion by spending hours and hours beating on their craft and then bringing that to the partnership.

To successfully practice on your own, you have to have exercises, know your routines individually, and have a regiment that you follow as with any workout. Practicing on your own can be difficult because as humans, we are typically self critical to the point where we convince ourselves to just wait for our partner or we believe we can't do it without our partner. This may be true for tricks or partner assisted moves, however; to be a champion you have to be the best individual dancer you can be and that in turn will make you a better dancer in the partnership. If asked, each coach is more than willing to provide you with technical, physical, and stretching exercises to help you improve and make your personal practice time more productive.

Don't forget to set up your practice time using impractical, semi-practical, and practical types of practicing. If you would like, you can set up your practice schedule using the five different elements as we discussed earlier.

QUESTIONS AND ANSWERS

Throughout the week you will also find that you have questions that you want to ask at your lesson. WRITE them down and at the beginning of your next lesson ask your coach. . . After it gets answered, be sure to write down the answer so you can refer to it at any time. This creates another valuable resource for your success.

WATCHING VIDEOS

Using your resources is very important! In this day and age, you have access to the top dancers in the world in a matter of seconds. You may choose at times to watch the professionals strictly as entertainment. At other times, it is imperative that you watch the top dancers in the world for the sole purpose of learning from what they do right!

REMEMBER—YouTube videos are a tool to help improve your dancing but YouTube cannot teach you how to dance.

Here are a few things you can do to make your video watching productive:

a) Pick on of the things you are working on in your dancing and go look for it.

For example, if you are working on rumba walks, go and watch one of the top dancers and look for their rumba walks in their routine and how they execute them.

b) Use a 3x5 notecard to cover up the area that you are not watching to keep your focus on what you are watching.

When wanting to watch footwork, cover up everything but the dancers feet so you can stay focused on what you are trying to watch.

c) Watch the video first and then pick out things you want to look at the second time you watch it.

Watching a video once lets you enjoy the entertainment value and then after, you can look for the things you are learning in your lessons or working on in practice.

HOW TO WATCH PRACTICE VIDEOS

You and your partner work on a lot of things in practice. How can you be sure you are executing the things you are learning? How can you make sure your dancing looks the way it feels? This is where videoing comes in!

When you are in practice, have someone record your dancing so you can analyze it. Watching videos helps you realize what your dancing looks like and can bring up questions that you can bring to your main coach. Be constructive and positive when critiquing your videos. Focus on what you personally can do before looking at your partner.

VIDEOING IS VERY IMPORTANT! MAKE IT A WEEKLY PRIORITY TO PUT VIDEOING INTO YOUR PRACTICE SCHEDULE.

When you video at your practice, don't be afraid to look at the positive side of your dancing as well. Seeing your improvement is always good but it is also good to see what you need to do better. Pictures are important too. Taking pictures of frame, positions, posture, etc. helps you see what your dancing looks like. Keep the pictures as future reference to see improvement and to see what you are learning.

Videoing is very important! Make it a weekly priority to put videoing into your practice schedule.

COMPETITIONS

"The principle is competing against yourself. It's about self-improvement, about being better than you were the day before."

-Steve Young

DEDICATED
ATHLETIC
NEVER GIVES UP
CONTROLLED
EMOTIONAL

COMPETITION

Competing is an exciting part of what we do. It can leave you excited and pumped for the next competition or it can leave you devastated and not wanting to do it ever again. Part of your growth as a dancer will be to learn how to handle yourself in both scenarios of massive success and utter disappointment. One thing is certain, you will win some and you will lose some. That being said there are a few things that can help you improve your ability to be competitive and get noticed positively while you are on the floor. To be specific we will focus on three main factors that are must haves for competition.

First is your "IT" factor. Your "IT" factor encompasses many things in which you will learn about through the years but essentially it is your ability to perform, your appearance, and your overall presence on the floor. This element of your dancing is massively important! Without a strong "IT" factor you could have wonderful technique and clean dancing and still not make the next round of callbacks. It is the first thing judges will notice about you and in many cases they will not even consider you for the next round unless your "IT" factor stands out amongst the crowd.

YOUR "IT" FACTOR . . . IS YOUR ABILITY TO PERFORM, YOUR APPEARANCE, AND YOUR OVERALL PRESENCE ON THE FLOOR.

The next factor is your skill level. Your skill level includes your ballroom technique and your overall dance technique. These things combine to make up your overall technical ability. The process of improving this factor takes time, dedication, repetition, attention to detail, and constant improvement. At a certain stage in competition when the "IT" factors of you and your competitors become comparable your skill level will become the determining factor. It is certainly possible at a certain point that your skill level is so much greater that someone with less skill and a good "IT" factor can no longer beat you.

The last factor necessary is your connections. Who you know and who knows you. If a judge has seen you at enough competitions or even knows your name due to having taught you before, it makes it much easier for them to recognize you on the floor. Remember in early rounds of competition a judge may only have about 7.5 seconds to look at you and

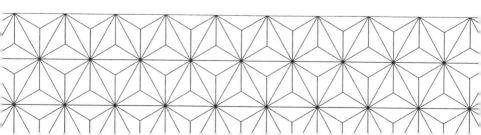

make their decision. Clearly this factor is more important the higher up in the ranks you get, however, for a while in the early stages of your dancing this factor won't play as large of a role in your progress. As it becomes more important you will begin to learn how to go about improving this element of your progression.

I believe these three factors are very important in the order presented. While some in the dance community may place different priorities on each of these factors, It is important to remember that regardless of the order of importance all three of these factors will determine your success in competitive dancing.

COSTUMING AND GROOMING

You put a lot of time, money, and energy into your dancing. It is important that your costuming reflects all of your hard work! Research how the top couples are branding themselves and fit that into your own style.

Costuming

Ladies: Here are a few tips when considering costuming.

- Know what colors look good on you.
- Ask your coach what your assets are and design or choose a costume that shows them off!
- Pick 1 or 2 styles you like and stick to them. When you try to put too many things into one dress it can end poorly.

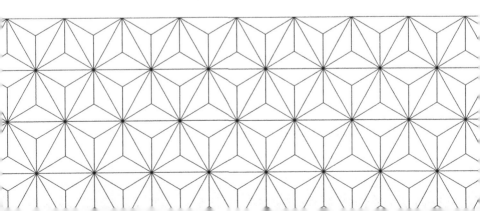

Men:
- Look at what the pros are wearing—the trends change frequently.
- Tailsuits and smooth suits must fit you well! If it doesn't fit you well, it will affect your results!!

Both:
- Consult your coach on every step of choosing, renting or designing a new costume.

HAIR AND MAKEUP

This is all about trial and error. Practice makes perfect...just try not to practice on competition days.

- Find someone you trust to help you with your hair and makeup for competitions!
- Girls you must know how to do a low bun or a basic hairstyle yourself!
- Boys you must know how to do your hair yourself!

There are plenty of people that are experts at doing hair and makeup if you would like to hire them. There are also tutorials on Youtube that are easily found with minimal research.

TANNING

Boys and girls both need to be tan! Tanning is very important in order to not be out of place and look like you are dead from all of the bright lights. The lights tend to drown you out. Consult your coach about what is the best tanning method for you based on the style you are dancing.

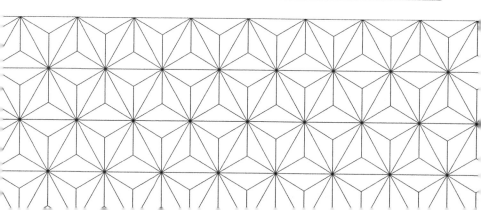

"NO MATTER HOW YOU FEEL, GET UP, DRESS UP, SHOW UP, AND NEVER GIVE UP."

-ANONYMOUS

Below you will find a list of essential hair/makeup products and brands that we have found to work the best:

Hairspray
Got 2 be Glued Hairspray

Silhouette Hairspray

Hair
Bobby Pins

Bristle Brush (Slicking Brush)

Comb

Hair Nets (one that matches your hair)

Mousse

Shine Spray

Thick Hair Ties

U Pins

Make-up
Blush

Bronzer

Clear Elmer's Glue for Rhinestones in hair

Dark colored eye shadow-colors that compliment your eye color

Eyebrow liner/filler

Eyelash glue

Eyeliner

Fake Nails

False eyelashes

Foundation

Lip liner

Lipstick

Makeup Bag

Mascara

Nail Glue

Primer

Q-tips

Tanning

White eyeshadow (MAC is the best brand)

Tanning
Aerie Jo

Bare minerals

MAC tanning spray

Pro tan(Amazon)

Sex Symbol

Spray Tan

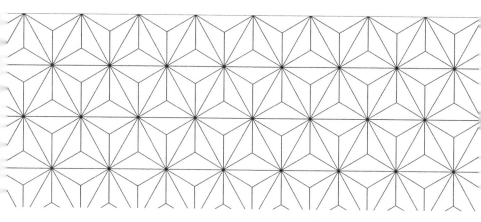

COMPETITION PREPARATION

The week and day of competitions are unpredictable. Everything may go perfectly or you may have a curve ball thrown at you. You can't necessarily control if you are sick or if your shoe breaks at the competition, but you can make sure that everything within your control is in order. Visualization is the first step in making sure that everything is going to go how you want it to go. Visualize getting ready and your hair and makeup working perfectly. Visualize your costume fitting just how it should. Visualize your warm-up. Visualize the round feeling amazing.

The week of the comp:

Do rounds every day: Remember you can control the amount of stamina that you have out on the floor if you prepare properly.

Get into performance mode: Focus on your "It" factor. By this point it is going to be difficult to change technique.

Make a checklist: Make sure all of the little things are in order (costumes, shoes, makeup, hair, nails, etc...)

Plan your competition warm-up: Plan this like your daily practice. How many rounds are you doing? When are you getting dressed? How long before your event are you meeting?

Videotape your event: Plan to have someone video you at the competition (see *How to Watch your Competition Videos*)

The day of the comp:

1. Eat a good breakfast and make sure you have enough food to keep you energized throughout the day, however you want your body to have consistency. For example if you never eat a big breakfast, don't start the day of the competition.

2. Boys make sure to laminate your number. You can either take it somewhere or buy laminating paper that you keep with you competition stuff.

3. Decide specifically when and where you are going to meet your partner before your event.

4. Follow your competition warm-up schedule that you set previously.

5. Warm-up in a similar way that you do in practice do things that your mind and body are used to doing.

6. Do rounds before you go onto the floor- your first round of the day should NEVER be on the competition floor. You should be sweating!

Example of how to set up a competition practice schedule:

If you meet two hours before:

Block of time:	What:
15 min.	Stretch on your own and do your technical exercises.
15 min.	Get connected with your partner physically and mentally
15 min.	Round
30 min.	Get dressed
15 min.	Round
Remainder of time:	Stay connected and leave your parents, friends(boyfriends/girlfriends included), and siblings out of your space.

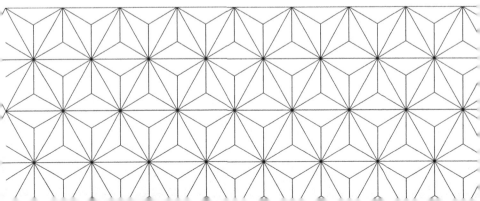

Checklist for competitions
(All styles included):

Boys

- ☐ Tailsuit
- ☐ Tail shirt 1
- ☐ Tail shirt 2
- ☐ Studs
- ☐ Neck studs
- ☐ Cuff links
- ☐ Bow tie
- ☐ Waist coat
- ☐ Handkerchief
- ☐ Suspenders
- ☐ Under shirt
- ☐ Jacket
- ☐ Pants
- ☐ Tupperware for tail suit accessories
- ☐ Super Glue
- ☐ Latin costume
- ☐ Smooth Suit
- ☐ Shoes (Latin and standard)
- ☐ Black socks
- ☐ Makeup
- ☐ Hair stuff
- ☐ Towel
- ☐ Warm-up clothes
- ☐ Music
- ☐ Robe/Jacket
- ☐ Lamentation Paper
- ☐ Safety Pins

Girls

- ☐ Latin Costume
- ☐ Standard Costume
- ☐ Smooth Costume
- ☐ Accessories (earrings, bracelets, necklaces, etc.)
- ☐ Shoes (Latin, standard, and smooth)
- ☐ Nail glue/Super glue
- ☐ E6000
- ☐ Makeup (All of it!)
- ☐ Hair stuff (hair pins, hair ties, hairspray, hairnets, combs, slicking brush, etc.)
- ☐ Fake eyelashes
- ☐ Fishnets
- ☐ Warm-up clothes
- ☐ Music
- ☐ Tanning stuff
- ☐ Robe/Jacket
- ☐ Safety pins
- ☐ Sewing Kit

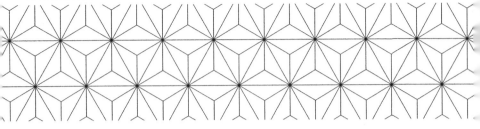

"COMPETE YOUR HARDEST. DREAM YOUR BIGGEST. BE YOUR GREATEST."

-UNKOWN

COMPETITION PLANNING

Competitions are a place for your hard work to be judged by experienced adjudicators. There are local competitions and then there are out of state competitions. Many of the high schools and universities put on competitions. Smaller competitions are great for experience and floor time. Local competitions allow you to learn how competitions are run and become familiar with the process. As your dancing improves and you continue to do local competitions, the time will come for you to travel to competitions outside of your state. These increase your branding and your knowledge of the dancers in other states. In addition, out of state competitions give you more experience.

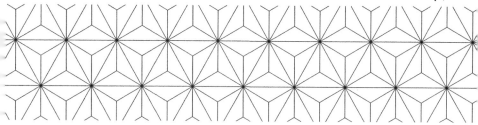

COMPETITION SIZE

There are three different types of competitions: small, medium, and large.

Small competitions generally do not have large attendance. These competitions are good for floor time and it gives you an opportunity to put on the floor what you have been working on in your lessons. Small competitions are great for getting video for you to improve with.

Medium competitions will have more of your competitors. These competitions will help you start to develop floorcraft, as there will be more couples in the events, and will give you a chance to compete in front of a bigger audience.

Big competitions will have all of your main competitors and most experienced judges. These competitions allow you to present your brand as a couple. You will get to compete against the main circle of your competitors and gain valuable information from the results about where your dancing is and what you can do to ultimately progress in your division.

It is important that you attend as many competitions as possible. The competition setting and atmosphere is much different than practice and it allows you, through video, to see the little things that need to be done to improve your dancing. It also allows your main coach to see what improvements need to be made. Competitions give you a chance to set goals and give you something to work for. Talk with your main coach about the best competitions for you and your partner to attend, and make sure you have clear reason for doing each competition.

TRAVELING TO COMPETITIONS

Traveling to competitions is a more expensive than doing competitions in your area because you have the extra expenses of hotel and transportation; however, out of state competitions are very beneficial. It allows you to get seen by many professional judges and gives you an opportunity to compete against couples from out of your area.

Preparing for out of state competitions is similar to an in state competition. You must register for the events in the style you are competing. Registration can be done by searching the name of the competition and then going to the main site and getting the form. Again, if you are not sure what events you should compete in, consult with your main coach.

TRAVELING TO COMPETITIONS ALLOWS YOU TO GET SEEN BY MANY PROFESSIONAL JUDGES AND GIVES YOU AN OPPORTUNITY TO COMPETE AGAINST COUPLES FROM OUT OF YOUR AREA

After you have registered, decide on transportation and hotel. Decide if you want to fly or drive and what is the best option for you and your expenses. If you drive, make sure that you get there in plenty of time before you compete. You can stay at the hotel the competition is held at or you can choose to stay at a hotel nearby. Make sure you and your partner have your hotel booked enough in advance before the competition.

You then need to look at your heat lists, those can be found on the site of the competition once everyone has registered. Make sure you plan to meet at least two hours before your event and that you warmup for all the styles you are competing in. Out of state competitions will usually have a smaller floor to warm up on near the main ballroom. You and your partner should have a warm up schedule written out before getting to the competition and that way, your warm up time is effective and gets you ready to compete. (See *Competition Preparation*)

When you go to any competition, make sure you are always dressed nice and look professional. First impressions are important and when you travel out of state, there is a chance that you will see and possibly talk to judges and professional coaches in attendance when you are not in your competition attire.

When you travel to a competition, make sure you have all parts to your costume and dance shoes. Double check everything before you leave and make sure you have all makeup and hair supplies. (Refer to the costuming section to find a checklist that you should look over before you leave.) When at the competition, you need to be ready in costume 30 minutes before you compete. You also need to make sure that you check in with the deck captain 30 minutes before the event starts. If your coach comes to the competition make sure you visit them in-between rounds.

Traveling to competitions is an exciting experience and will help your dancing immensely! It will also give you the experience needed to excel.

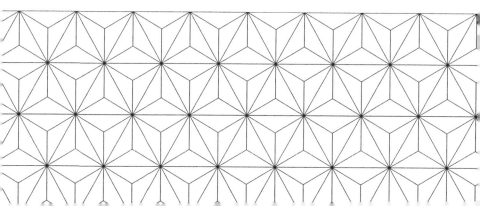

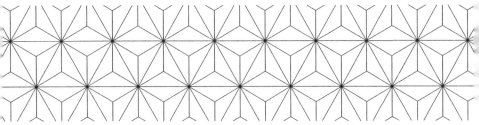

HOW TO WATCH YOUR COMPETITION VIDEOS

Watching your competition videos is important to your dancing. On the first day back to practice make sure this is the first thing you do together. Watch your videos for the things that you know how to fix along with the things that you want your coach to look at. Be specific in the things that you write down. Rather than saying that your arms are bad throughout, you can point out specific places you don't like so you can fix it. To make it easier for you set up a table that looks like the following. We have also included a chart in the workbook help you.

MAN	LADY	PARTNER-SHIP	COACH	WHAT I DID WELL
*In this column put things the man finds that he knows how to improve.	*In this column put things the lady finds that she knows how to improve.	*In this column put things you find together that you can improve on together.	*In this column put things for your coach to look at that you don't know how to fix on your own.	*In this column put all of the things that you did well.

When you have evaluated your videos make sure to allot time in your practice to work on your items in your list. Have this list ready to go for your lesson time. Be sure to add your findings to your practice schedule.

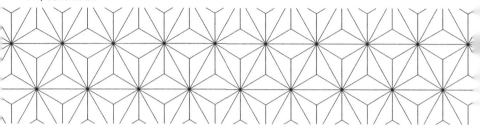

CONCLUSION

If you have made it to this point I would like to congratulate you on being one of the few people that choose to read to the end of a book. And I would like to present one last challenge. The information that I have presented has come from a full career and experience in ballroom dance and through executing and teaching many different approaches and methods. I have found that these methods have proven great results. By no means am I saying this is the only way that results can be attained, however I have found that it is one way that has proven to be effective. Therefore, my challenge to you is to commit to using the ideas and methods presented in this book for at least a month in attempt to see how they work for you. I have found many times that the couples that give up on things like the practice schedule too early end up with a watered down success and many more challenges within their partnership. As with anything greatness is achieved by constant and never ending improvement. The information I have shared with you I believe will help you to improve in a consistent manner. I have included a dance journal after this for you to utilize the skills presented in this book. If you use all of the pages in the journal or you get a new partner, you can get the dance journal seperately.

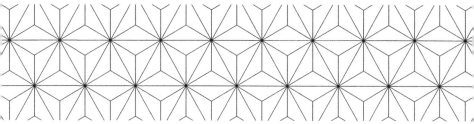

    I wish you all the best in your journey in ballroom dance and I invite you to contact me with any questions you may have concerning the information I have shared with you. Good luck, best wishes and don't forget to find your "majic" everyday!

Michael A. Johnson

WELCOME TO THE GRIND

"The battle royale between you and your mind, your body and the devil on your shoulder telling you this is just a waste of time."

-Unknown

CONTENTS

- **CREATE YOUR PARTNERSHIP**
- **COMPETITION PLANNING**
- **COMPETITION VIDEOS**
- **PLANNING PRACTICE**

HOW TO USE THIS JOURNAL

This journal is intended to be used to help you improve your practice time through years of development and trial and error I have discovered the methods that have been most effective in improving your skills in practice time. Many of the ideas and concepts in this journal are self explanatory, however if you would like a more in depth explanation on each of the sections in this journal please refer to "The First Step: A Guide to Competitive Ballroom Dancing"

CREATE YOUR PARTNERSHIP

"Vision without action is a daydream. Action without vision is a nightmare."

-Japanese Proverb

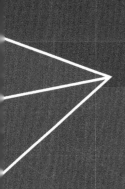

ESTABLISH YOUR GOALS

The way you describe your goals can change your mindset and out-look. Describe your goals as reasonable and lofty in order to push yourself enough to be able to succeed.

INDIVIDUAL GOALS

_____
_____
_____
_____
_____
_____
_____
_____
_____
_____
_____
_____

PARTNERSHIP GOALS

_____
_____
_____
_____
_____
_____
_____
_____
_____
_____
_____
_____
_____

CREATE YOUR PARTNERSHIP

Decide who is going to make up your team, how many lessons you are going to have each week, the amount of time you are going to practice, and the competitions you will compete at.

STYLES

Ballroom   Latin   Smooth   Rhythm

LEVELS

Junior   Youth Prechamp   Youth

Adult Novice   Prechamp   Under 21   Amateur

LESSON BUDGET

Per Week: _____   Incoming Coaches: _____

Technique Classes: _____

PRACTICE TIME

Daily: _____   Weekly: _____

COSTUMING/PRACTICE ATTIRE

Man: _____   Woman: _____

GOALS:

_____

_____

_____

_____

COMPETITIONS

June: _____   Dec: _____

July: _____   Jan: _____

Aug: _____   Feb: _____

Sept: _____   Mar: _____

Oct: _____   April: _____

Nov: _____   May: _____

SIGNATURES

Man: _____   Woman: _____

COMPETITION PLANNING

"Strategy without tactics is the slowest route to victory."

-Sun Tzu

Use these two pages to prepare for your competition. Below is a list of things we believe you will need along with space to add your own items if there is something you need that we haven't included. The next page includes a chart for you to create your warm-up schedule.

Checklist for competitions

(All styles included):

Boys	Girls
☐ Tailsuit	☐ Latin Costume
☐ Tail shirt 1	☐ Standard Costume
☐ Tail shirt 2	☐ Smooth Costume
☐ Studs	☐ Accessories (earrings, brace-lets, necklaces, etc.)
☐ Neck studs	
☐ Cuff links	☐ Shoes (Latin, standard, and smooth)
☐ Bow tie	
☐ Waist coat	☐ Nail glue/Super glue
☐ Handkerchief	☐ E6000
☐ Suspenders	☐ Makeup (All of it!)
☐ Under shirt	☐ Hair stuff (hair pins, hair ties, hairspray, hairnets, combs, slicking brush, etc.)
☐ Jacket	
☐ Pants	
☐ Tupperware for tail suit accessories	☐ Fake eyelashes
	☐ Fishnets
☐ Super Glue	☐ Warm-up clothes
☐ Latin costume	☐ Music
☐ Smooth Suit	☐ Tanning stuff
☐ Shoes (Latin and standard)	☐ Robe/Jacket
☐ Black socks	☐ Safety pins
☐ Makeup	☐ Sewing Kit
☐ Hair stuff	☐
☐ Towel	☐
☐ Warm-up clothes	☐
☐ Music	☐
☐ Robe/Jacket	☐
☐ Lamentation Paper	☐
☐ Safety Pins	☐
☐	☐
☐	☐
☐	☐
☐	☐
☐	☐
☐	☐
☐	☐

COMPETITION PLANNING

Date: _____

Competition: _____

Warm-up Schedule

TIME	WHAT

Use these two pages to prepare for your competition. Below is a list of things we believe you will need along with space to add your own items if there is something you need that we haven't included. The next page includes a chart for you to create your warm-up schedule.

Checklist for competitions
(All styles included):

Boys
- ☐ Tailsuit
- ☐ Tail shirt 1
- ☐ Tail shirt 2
- ☐ Studs
- ☐ Neck studs
- ☐ Cuff links
- ☐ Bow tie
- ☐ Waist coat
- ☐ Handkerchief
- ☐ Suspenders
- ☐ Under shirt
- ☐ Jacket
- ☐ Pants
- ☐ Tupperware for tail suit accessories
- ☐ Super Glue
- ☐ Latin costume
- ☐ Smooth Suit
- ☐ Shoes (Latin and standard)
- ☐ Black socks
- ☐ Makeup
- ☐ Hair stuff
- ☐ Towel
- ☐ Warm-up clothes
- ☐ Music
- ☐ Robe/Jacket
- ☐ Lamentation Paper
- ☐ Safety Pins
- ☐
- ☐
- ☐
- ☐
- ☐
- ☐
- ☐

Girls
- ☐ Latin Costume
- ☐ Standard Costume
- ☐ Smooth Costume
- ☐ Accessories (earrings, bracelets, necklaces, etc.)
- ☐ Shoes (Latin, standard, and smooth)
- ☐ Nail glue/Super glue
- ☐ E6000
- ☐ Makeup (All of it!)
- ☐ Hair stuff (hair pins, hair ties, hairspray, hairnets, combs, slicking brush, etc.)
- ☐ Fake eyelashes
- ☐ Fishnets
- ☐ Warm-up clothes
- ☐ Music
- ☐ Tanning stuff
- ☐ Robe/Jacket
- ☐ Safety pins
- ☐ Sewing Kit
- ☐
- ☐
- ☐
- ☐
- ☐
- ☐
- ☐
- ☐
- ☐
- ☐
- ☐
- ☐
- ☐

COMPETITION PLANNING

Date: _____

Competition: _____

Warm-up Schedule

TIME	WHAT

Use these two pages to prepare for your competition. Below is a list of things we believe you will need along with space to add your own items if there is something you need that we haven't included. The next page includes a chart for you to create your warm-up schedule.

Checklist for competitions
(All styles included):

Boys
- ☐ Tailsuit
- ☐ Tail shirt 1
- ☐ Tail shirt 2
- ☐ Studs
- ☐ Neck studs
- ☐ Cuff links
- ☐ Bow tie
- ☐ Waist coat
- ☐ Handkerchief
- ☐ Suspenders
- ☐ Under shirt
- ☐ Jacket
- ☐ Pants
- ☐ Tupperware for tail suit accessories
- ☐ Super Glue
- ☐ Latin costume
- ☐ Smooth Suit
- ☐ Shoes (Latin and standard)
- ☐ Black socks
- ☐ Makeup
- ☐ Hair stuff
- ☐ Towel
- ☐ Warm-up clothes
- ☐ Music
- ☐ Robe/Jacket
- ☐ Lamentation Paper
- ☐ Safety Pins
- ☐
- ☐
- ☐
- ☐
- ☐
- ☐
- ☐

Girls
- ☐ Latin Costume
- ☐ Standard Costume
- ☐ Smooth Costume
- ☐ Accessories (earrings, bracelets, necklaces, etc.)
- ☐ Shoes (Latin, standard, and smooth)
- ☐ Nail glue/Super glue
- ☐ E6000
- ☐ Makeup (All of it!)
- ☐ Hair stuff (hair pins, hair ties, hairspray, hairnets, combs, slicking brush, etc.)
- ☐ Fake eyelashes
- ☐ Fishnets
- ☐ Warm-up clothes
- ☐ Music
- ☐ Tanning stuff
- ☐ Robe/Jacket
- ☐ Safety pins
- ☐ Sewing Kit
- ☐
- ☐
- ☐
- ☐
- ☐
- ☐
- ☐
- ☐
- ☐
- ☐
- ☐
- ☐
- ☐

COMPETITION PLANNING

Date: _____

Competition: _____

Warm-up Schedule

TIME	WHAT

Use these two pages to prepare for your competition. Below is a list of things we believe you will need along with space to add your own items if there is something you need that we haven't included. The next page includes a chart for you to create your warm-up schedule.

Checklist for competitions

(All styles included):

Boys
- ☐ Tailsuit
- ☐ Tail shirt 1
- ☐ Tail shirt 2
- ☐ Studs
- ☐ Neck studs
- ☐ Cuff links
- ☐ Bow tie
- ☐ Waist coat
- ☐ Handkerchief
- ☐ Suspenders
- ☐ Under shirt
- ☐ Jacket
- ☐ Pants
- ☐ Tupperware for tail suit accessories
- ☐ Super Glue
- ☐ Latin costume
- ☐ Smooth Suit
- ☐ Shoes (Latin and standard)
- ☐ Black socks
- ☐ Makeup
- ☐ Hair stuff
- ☐ Towel
- ☐ Warm-up clothes
- ☐ Music
- ☐ Robe/Jacket
- ☐ Lamentation Paper
- ☐ Safety Pins
- ☐
- ☐
- ☐
- ☐
- ☐
- ☐
- ☐

Girls
- ☐ Latin Costume
- ☐ Standard Costume
- ☐ Smooth Costume
- ☐ Accessories (earrings, bracelets, necklaces, etc.)
- ☐ Shoes (Latin, standard, and smooth)
- ☐ Nail glue/Super glue
- ☐ E6000
- ☐ Makeup (All of it!)
- ☐ Hair stuff (hair pins, hair ties, hairspray, hairnets, combs, slicking brush, etc.)
- ☐ Fake eyelashes
- ☐ Fishnets
- ☐ Warm-up clothes
- ☐ Music
- ☐ Tanning stuff
- ☐ Robe/Jacket
- ☐ Safety pins
- ☐ Sewing Kit
- ☐
- ☐
- ☐
- ☐
- ☐
- ☐
- ☐
- ☐
- ☐
- ☐
- ☐
- ☐
- ☐

COMPETITION PLANNING

Date: _____

Competition: _____

Warm-up Schedule

TIME	WHAT

Use these two pages to prepare for your competition. Below is a list of things we believe you will need along with space to add your own items if there is something you need that we haven't included. The next page includes a chart for you to create your warm-up schedule.

Checklist for competitions
(All styles included):

Boys
- ☐ Tailsuit
- ☐ Tail shirt 1
- ☐ Tail shirt 2
- ☐ Studs
- ☐ Neck studs
- ☐ Cuff links
- ☐ Bow tie
- ☐ Waist coat
- ☐ Handkerchief
- ☐ Suspenders
- ☐ Under shirt
- ☐ Jacket
- ☐ Pants
- ☐ Tupperware for tail suit accessories
- ☐ Super Glue
- ☐ Latin costume
- ☐ Smooth Suit
- ☐ Shoes (Latin and standard)
- ☐ Black socks
- ☐ Makeup
- ☐ Hair stuff
- ☐ Towel
- ☐ Warm-up clothes
- ☐ Music
- ☐ Robe/Jacket
- ☐ Lamentation Paper
- ☐ Safety Pins
- ☐
- ☐
- ☐
- ☐
- ☐
- ☐
- ☐

Girls
- ☐ Latin Costume
- ☐ Standard Costume
- ☐ Smooth Costume
- ☐ Accessories (earrings, bracelets, necklaces, etc.)
- ☐ Shoes (Latin, standard, and smooth)
- ☐ Nail glue/Super glue
- ☐ E6000
- ☐ Makeup (All of it!)
- ☐ Hair stuff (hair pins, hair ties, hairspray, hairnets, combs, slicking brush, etc.)
- ☐ Fake eyelashes
- ☐ Fishnets
- ☐ Warm-up clothes
- ☐ Music
- ☐ Tanning stuff
- ☐ Robe/Jacket
- ☐ Safety pins
- ☐ Sewing Kit
- ☐
- ☐
- ☐
- ☐
- ☐
- ☐
- ☐
- ☐
- ☐
- ☐
- ☐
- ☐
- ☐

COMPETITION PLANNING

Date: _____

Competition: _____

Warm-up Schedule

TIME	WHAT

Use these two pages to prepare for your competition. Below is a list of things we believe you will need along with space to add your own items if there is something you need that we haven't included. The next page includes a chart for you to create your warm-up schedule.

Checklist for competitions
(All styles included):

Boys
- ☐ Tailsuit
- ☐ Tail shirt 1
- ☐ Tail shirt 2
- ☐ Studs
- ☐ Neck studs
- ☐ Cuff links
- ☐ Bow tie
- ☐ Waist coat
- ☐ Handkerchief
- ☐ Suspenders
- ☐ Under shirt
- ☐ Jacket
- ☐ Pants
- ☐ Tupperware for tail suit accessories
- ☐ Super Glue
- ☐ Latin costume
- ☐ Smooth Suit
- ☐ Shoes (Latin and standard)
- ☐ Black socks
- ☐ Makeup
- ☐ Hair stuff
- ☐ Towel
- ☐ Warm-up clothes
- ☐ Music
- ☐ Robe/Jacket
- ☐ Lamentation Paper
- ☐ Safety Pins
- ☐
- ☐
- ☐
- ☐
- ☐
- ☐
- ☐

Girls
- ☐ Latin Costume
- ☐ Standard Costume
- ☐ Smooth Costume
- ☐ Accessories (earrings, bracelets, necklaces, etc.)
- ☐ Shoes (Latin, standard, and smooth)
- ☐ Nail glue/Super glue
- ☐ E6000
- ☐ Makeup (All of it!)
- ☐ Hair stuff (hair pins, hair ties, hairspray, hairnets, combs, slicking brush, etc.)
- ☐ Fake eyelashes
- ☐ Fishnets
- ☐ Warm-up clothes
- ☐ Music
- ☐ Tanning stuff
- ☐ Robe/Jacket
- ☐ Safety pins
- ☐ Sewing Kit
- ☐
- ☐
- ☐
- ☐
- ☐
- ☐
- ☐
- ☐
- ☐
- ☐
- ☐
- ☐
- ☐

COMPETITION PLANNING

Date: _____

Competition: _____

Warm-up Schedule

TIME	WHAT

Use these two pages to prepare for your competition. Below is a list of things we believe you will need along with space to add your own items if there is something you need that we haven't included. The next page includes a chart for you to create your warm-up schedule.

Checklist for competitions
(All styles included):

Boys
- ☐ Tailsuit
- ☐ Tail shirt 1
- ☐ Tail shirt 2
- ☐ Studs
- ☐ Neck studs
- ☐ Cuff links
- ☐ Bow tie
- ☐ Waist coat
- ☐ Handkerchief
- ☐ Suspenders
- ☐ Under shirt
- ☐ Jacket
- ☐ Pants
- ☐ Tupperware for tail suit accessories
- ☐ Super Glue
- ☐ Latin costume
- ☐ Smooth Suit
- ☐ Shoes (Latin and standard)
- ☐ Black socks
- ☐ Makeup
- ☐ Hair stuff
- ☐ Towel
- ☐ Warm-up clothes
- ☐ Music
- ☐ Robe/Jacket
- ☐ Lamentation Paper
- ☐ Safety Pins
- ☐
- ☐
- ☐
- ☐
- ☐
- ☐
- ☐

Girls
- ☐ Latin Costume
- ☐ Standard Costume
- ☐ Smooth Costume
- ☐ Accessories (earrings, bracelets, necklaces, etc.)
- ☐ Shoes (Latin, standard, and smooth)
- ☐ Nail glue/Super glue
- ☐ E6000
- ☐ Makeup (All of it!)
- ☐ Hair stuff (hair pins, hair ties, hairspray, hairnets, combs, slicking brush, etc.)
- ☐ Fake eyelashes
- ☐ Fishnets
- ☐ Warm-up clothes
- ☐ Music
- ☐ Tanning stuff
- ☐ Robe/Jacket
- ☐ Safety pins
- ☐ Sewing Kit
- ☐
- ☐
- ☐
- ☐
- ☐
- ☐
- ☐
- ☐
- ☐
- ☐
- ☐

COMPETITION PLANNING

Date: _____

Competition: _____

Warm-up Schedule

TIME	WHAT

Use these two pages to prepare for your competition. Below is a list of things we believe you will need along with space to add your own items if there is something you need that we haven't included. The next page includes a chart for you to create your warm-up schedule.

Checklist for competitions
(All styles included):

Boys
- ☐ Tailsuit
- ☐ Tail shirt 1
- ☐ Tail shirt 2
- ☐ Studs
- ☐ Neck studs
- ☐ Cuff links
- ☐ Bow tie
- ☐ Waist coat
- ☐ Handkerchief
- ☐ Suspenders
- ☐ Under shirt
- ☐ Jacket
- ☐ Pants
- ☐ Tupperware for tail suit accessories
- ☐ Super Glue
- ☐ Latin costume
- ☐ Smooth Suit
- ☐ Shoes (Latin and standard)
- ☐ Black socks
- ☐ Makeup
- ☐ Hair stuff
- ☐ Towel
- ☐ Warm-up clothes
- ☐ Music
- ☐ Robe/Jacket
- ☐ Lamentation Paper
- ☐ Safety Pins
- ☐
- ☐
- ☐
- ☐
- ☐
- ☐
- ☐

Girls
- ☐ Latin Costume
- ☐ Standard Costume
- ☐ Smooth Costume
- ☐ Accessories (earrings, bracelets, necklaces, etc.)
- ☐ Shoes (Latin, standard, and smooth)
- ☐ Nail glue/Super glue
- ☐ E6000
- ☐ Makeup (All of it!)
- ☐ Hair stuff (hair pins, hair ties, hairspray, hairnets, combs, slicking brush, etc.)
- ☐ Fake eyelashes
- ☐ Fishnets
- ☐ Warm-up clothes
- ☐ Music
- ☐ Tanning stuff
- ☐ Robe/Jacket
- ☐ Safety pins
- ☐ Sewing Kit
- ☐
- ☐
- ☐
- ☐
- ☐
- ☐
- ☐
- ☐
- ☐
- ☐
- ☐
- ☐

COMPETITION PLANNING

Date: _____

Competition: _____

Warm-up Schedule

TIME	WHAT

Use these two pages to prepare for your competition. Below is a list of things we believe you will need along with space to add your own items if there is something you need that we haven't included. The next page includes a chart for you to create your warm-up schedule.

Checklist for competitions
(All styles included):

Boys
- ☐ Tailsuit
- ☐ Tail shirt 1
- ☐ Tail shirt 2
- ☐ Studs
- ☐ Neck studs
- ☐ Cuff links
- ☐ Bow tie
- ☐ Waist coat
- ☐ Handkerchief
- ☐ Suspenders
- ☐ Under shirt
- ☐ Jacket
- ☐ Pants
- ☐ Tupperware for tail suit accessories
- ☐ Super Glue
- ☐ Latin costume
- ☐ Smooth Suit
- ☐ Shoes (Latin and standard)
- ☐ Black socks
- ☐ Makeup
- ☐ Hair stuff
- ☐ Towel
- ☐ Warm-up clothes
- ☐ Music
- ☐ Robe/Jacket
- ☐ Lamentation Paper
- ☐ Safety Pins
- ☐
- ☐
- ☐
- ☐
- ☐
- ☐
- ☐

Girls
- ☐ Latin Costume
- ☐ Standard Costume
- ☐ Smooth Costume
- ☐ Accessories (earrings, bracelets, necklaces, etc.)
- ☐ Shoes (Latin, standard, and smooth)
- ☐ Nail glue/Super glue
- ☐ E6000
- ☐ Makeup (All of it!)
- ☐ Hair stuff (hair pins, hair ties, hairspray, hairnets, combs, slicking brush, etc.)
- ☐ Fake eyelashes
- ☐ Fishnets
- ☐ Warm-up clothes
- ☐ Music
- ☐ Tanning stuff
- ☐ Robe/Jacket
- ☐ Safety pins
- ☐ Sewing Kit
- ☐
- ☐
- ☐
- ☐
- ☐
- ☐
- ☐
- ☐
- ☐
- ☐
- ☐
- ☐
- ☐
- ☐

COMPETITION PLANNING

Date: _____

Competition: _____

Warm-up Schedule

TIME	WHAT

Use these two pages to prepare for your competition. Below is a list of things we believe you will need along with space to add your own items if there is something you need that we haven't included. The next page includes a chart for you to create your warm-up schedule.

Checklist for competitions

(All styles included):

Boys
- ☐ Tailsuit
- ☐ Tail shirt 1
- ☐ Tail shirt 2
- ☐ Studs
- ☐ Neck studs
- ☐ Cuff links
- ☐ Bow tie
- ☐ Waist coat
- ☐ Handkerchief
- ☐ Suspenders
- ☐ Under shirt
- ☐ Jacket
- ☐ Pants
- ☐ Tupperware for tail suit accessories
- ☐ Super Glue
- ☐ Latin costume
- ☐ Smooth Suit
- ☐ Shoes (Latin and standard)
- ☐ Black socks
- ☐ Makeup
- ☐ Hair stuff
- ☐ Towel
- ☐ Warm-up clothes
- ☐ Music
- ☐ Robe/Jacket
- ☐ Lamentation Paper
- ☐ Safety Pins
- ☐
- ☐
- ☐
- ☐
- ☐
- ☐
- ☐

Girls
- ☐ Latin Costume
- ☐ Standard Costume
- ☐ Smooth Costume
- ☐ Accessories (earrings, bracelets, necklaces, etc.)
- ☐ Shoes (Latin, standard, and smooth)
- ☐ Nail glue/Super glue
- ☐ E6000
- ☐ Makeup (All of it!)
- ☐ Hair stuff (hair pins, hair ties, hairspray, hairnets, combs, slicking brush, etc.)
- ☐ Fake eyelashes
- ☐ Fishnets
- ☐ Warm-up clothes
- ☐ Music
- ☐ Tanning stuff
- ☐ Robe/Jacket
- ☐ Safety pins
- ☐ Sewing Kit
- ☐
- ☐
- ☐
- ☐
- ☐
- ☐
- ☐
- ☐
- ☐
- ☐
- ☐
- ☐
- ☐

COMPETITION PLANNING
Date: _____
Competition: _____

Warm-up Schedule

TIME	WHAT

Use these two pages to prepare for your competition. Below is a list of things we believe you will need along with space to add your own items if there is something you need that we haven't included. The next page includes a chart for you to create your warm-up schedule.

Checklist for competitions
(All styles included):

Boys
- ☐ Tailsuit
- ☐ Tail shirt 1
- ☐ Tail shirt 2
- ☐ Studs
- ☐ Neck studs
- ☐ Cuff links
- ☐ Bow tie
- ☐ Waist coat
- ☐ Handkerchief
- ☐ Suspenders
- ☐ Under shirt
- ☐ Jacket
- ☐ Pants
- ☐ Tupperware for tail suit accessories
- ☐ Super Glue
- ☐ Latin costume
- ☐ Smooth Suit
- ☐ Shoes (Latin and standard)
- ☐ Black socks
- ☐ Makeup
- ☐ Hair stuff
- ☐ Towel
- ☐ Warm-up clothes
- ☐ Music
- ☐ Robe/Jacket
- ☐ Lamentation Paper
- ☐ Safety Pins
- ☐
- ☐
- ☐
- ☐
- ☐
- ☐
- ☐

Girls
- ☐ Latin Costume
- ☐ Standard Costume
- ☐ Smooth Costume
- ☐ Accessories (earrings, bracelets, necklaces, etc.)
- ☐ Shoes (Latin, standard, and smooth)
- ☐ Nail glue/Super glue
- ☐ E6000
- ☐ Makeup (All of it!)
- ☐ Hair stuff (hair pins, hair ties, hairspray, hairnets, combs, slicking brush, etc.)
- ☐ Fake eyelashes
- ☐ Fishnets
- ☐ Warm-up clothes
- ☐ Music
- ☐ Tanning stuff
- ☐ Robe/Jacket
- ☐ Safety pins
- ☐ Sewing Kit
- ☐
- ☐
- ☐
- ☐
- ☐
- ☐
- ☐
- ☐
- ☐
- ☐
- ☐

COMPETITION PLANNING

Date: _____

Competition: _____

Warm-up Schedule

TIME	WHAT

Use these two pages to prepare for your competition. Below is a list of things we believe you will need along with space to add your own items if there is something you need that we haven't included. The next page includes a chart for you to create your warm-up schedule.

Checklist for competitions
(All styles included):

Boys
☐ Tailsuit
☐ Tail shirt 1
☐ Tail shirt 2
☐ Studs
☐ Neck studs
☐ Cuff links
☐ Bow tie
☐ Waist coat
☐ Handkerchief
☐ Suspenders
☐ Under shirt
☐ Jacket
☐ Pants
☐ Tupperware for tail suit accessories
☐ Super Glue
☐ Latin costume
☐ Smooth Suit
☐ Shoes (Latin and standard)
☐ Black socks
☐ Makeup
☐ Hair stuff
☐ Towel
☐ Warm-up clothes
☐ Music
☐ Robe/Jacket
☐ Lamentation Paper
☐ Safety Pins
☐
☐
☐
☐
☐
☐
☐

Girls
☐ Latin Costume
☐ Standard Costume
☐ Smooth Costume
☐ Accessories (earrings, bracelets, necklaces, etc.)
☐ Shoes (Latin, standard, and smooth)
☐ Nail glue/Super glue
☐ E6000
☐ Makeup (All of it!)
☐ Hair stuff (hair pins, hair ties, hairspray, hairnets, combs, slicking brush, etc.)
☐ Fake eyelashes
☐ Fishnets
☐ Warm-up clothes
☐ Music
☐ Tanning stuff
☐ Robe/Jacket
☐ Safety pins
☐ Sewing Kit
☐
☐
☐
☐
☐
☐
☐
☐
☐
☐
☐
☐

COMPETITION PLANNING

Date: _____

Competition: _____

Warm-up Schedule

TIME	WHAT

COMPETITION VIDEOS

"Proper film study is vital for any NFL team to win. Players that can take what they see on the screen and transfer that knowledge to the field will always have their "eyes on the prize."

-Marc Lillibridge

COMPETITION VIDEOS

Date: _____

Competition: _____

MAN	LADY	PARTNER-SHIP	COACH	WHAT I DID WELL

COMPETITION VIDEOS

Date: _____

Competition: _____

MAN	LADY	PARTNER-SHIP	COACH	WHAT I DID WELL

COMPETITION VIDEOS

Date: _____

Competition: _____

MAN	LADY	PARTNER-SHIP	COACH	WHAT I DID WELL

COMPETITION VIDEOS

Date: _____

Competition: _____

MAN	LADY	PARTNER-SHIP	COACH	WHAT I DID WELL

COMPETITION VIDEOS

Date: _____

Competition: _____

MAN	LADY	PARTNER-SHIP	COACH	WHAT I DID WELL

COMPETITION VIDEOS

Date: _____

Competition: _____

MAN	LADY	PARTNER-SHIP	COACH	WHAT I DID WELL

COMPETITION VIDEOS

Date: _____

Competition: _____

MAN	LADY	PARTNER-SHIP	COACH	WHAT I DID WELL

COMPETITION VIDEOS

Date: _____

Competition: _____

MAN	LADY	PARTNER-SHIP	COACH	WHAT I DID WELL

COMPETITION VIDEOS

Date: _____

Competition: _____

MAN	LADY	PARTNER-SHIP	COACH	WHAT I DID WELL

COMPETITION VIDEOS

Date: _____

Competition: _____

MAN	LADY	PARTNER-SHIP	COACH	WHAT I DID WELL

COMPETITION VIDEOS

Date: _____

Competition: _____

MAN	LADY	PARTNER-SHIP	COACH	WHAT I DID WELL

COMPETITION VIDEOS

Date: _____

Competition: _____

MAN	LADY	PARTNER-SHIP	COACH	WHAT I DID WELL

PLANNING YOUR PRACTICE

"While their competition is asleep, world-class leaders are up and they're not watching the news or reading the paper. They are thinking, planning and practicing."

-Robin S. Sharma

PLANNING PRACTICE

DATE: _____

DAYS UNTIL NATIONALS: _____

TIME	WHAT	FOCUS	TYPE	SUCCESS

DAILY NOTES/ QUESTIONS

_____
_____
_____
_____
_____
_____
_____
_____
_____
_____
_____
_____
_____
_____
_____
_____

TODAY'S MAJIC
Learn a latin syllabus
figure today.

PLANNING PRACTICE

DATE: _____

DAYS UNTIL NATIONALS: _____

TIME	WHAT	FOCUS	TYPE	SUCCESS

DAILY NOTES/ QUESTIONS

_____

_____

_____

_____

_____

_____

_____

_____

_____

_____

_____

_____

_____

_____

_____

_____

TODAY'S MAJIC
What's your favorite
dance today?

PLANNING PRACTICE

DATE: _____

DAYS UNTIL NATIONALS: _____

TIME	WHAT	FOCUS	TYPE	SUCCESS

DAILY NOTES/ QUESTIONS

_____
_____
_____
_____
_____
_____
_____
_____
_____
_____
_____
_____
_____
_____
_____
_____

TODAY'S MAJIC
What do love about your partner?

PLANNING PRACTICE

DATE: _____

DAYS UNTIL NATIONALS: _____

TIME	WHAT	FOCUS	TYPE	SUCCESS

DAILY NOTES/ QUESTIONS

_____
_____
_____
_____
_____
_____
_____
_____
_____
_____
_____
_____
_____
_____
_____
_____

TODAY'S MAJIC

Learn a standard syllabus figure today.

PLANNING PRACTICE

DATE: _____

DAYS UNTIL NATIONALS: _____

TIME	WHAT	FOCUS	TYPE	SUCCESS

DAILY NOTES/ QUESTIONS

_____
_____
_____
_____
_____
_____
_____
_____
_____
_____
_____
_____
_____
_____
_____
_____
_____
_____

TODAY'S MAJIC
Dance to your favorite song today.

PLANNING PRACTICE

DATE: _____

DAYS UNTIL NATIONALS: _____

TIME	WHAT	FOCUS	TYPE	SUCCESS

DAILY NOTES/ QUESTIONS

_____
_____
_____
_____
_____
_____
_____
_____
_____
_____
_____
_____
_____
_____
_____
_____
_____
_____

TODAY'S MAJIC

Learn a smooth syllabus figure today.

PLANNING PRACTICE

DATE: _____

DAYS UNTIL NATIONALS: _____

TIME	WHAT	FOCUS	TYPE	SUCCESS

DAILY NOTES/ QUESTIONS

_____
_____
_____
_____
_____
_____
_____
_____
_____
_____
_____
_____
_____
_____
_____
_____

TODAY'S MAJIC
What funny thing happened recently in practice?

PLANNING PRACTICE
DATE: _____
DAYS UNTIL NATIONALS: _____

TIME	WHAT	FOCUS	TYPE	SUCCESS

DAILY NOTES/ QUESTIONS
_____
_____
_____
_____
_____
_____
_____
_____
_____
_____
_____
_____
_____
_____
_____
_____
_____
_____

TODAY'S MAJIC
Learn a rhythm syllabus figure today.

PLANNING PRACTICE

DATE: _____

DAYS UNTIL NATIONALS: _____

TIME	WHAT	FOCUS	TYPE	SUCCESS

DAILY NOTES/ QUESTIONS

_____
_____
_____
_____
_____
_____
_____
_____
_____
_____
_____
_____
_____
_____
_____
_____
_____

TODAY'S MAJIC

What one thing do you want to improve in your dancing today?

PLANNING PRACTICE

DATE: _____

DAYS UNTIL NATIONALS: _____

TIME	WHAT	FOCUS	TYPE	SUCCESS

DAILY NOTES/ QUESTIONS

_____
_____
_____
_____
_____
_____
_____
_____
_____
_____
_____
_____
_____
_____
_____
_____

TODAY'S MAJIC
What do you appreciate
about your partner?

PLANNING PRACTICE

DATE: _____

DAYS UNTIL NATIONALS: _____

TIME	WHAT	FOCUS	TYPE	SUCCESS

DAILY NOTES/ QUESTIONS

_____
_____
_____
_____
_____
_____
_____
_____
_____
_____
_____
_____
_____
_____
_____
_____

TODAY'S MAJIC

Learn a standard syllabus figure today.

PLANNING PRACTICE

DATE: _____

DAYS UNTIL NATIONALS: _____

TIME	WHAT	FOCUS	TYPE	SUCCESS

DAILY NOTES/ QUESTIONS

_____
_____
_____
_____
_____
_____
_____
_____
_____
_____
_____
_____
_____
_____
_____
_____

TODAY'S MAJIC

What's your partner's favorite dance today?

PLANNING PRACTICE

DATE: _____

DAYS UNTIL NATIONALS: _____

TIME	WHAT	FOCUS	TYPE	SUCCESS

DAILY NOTES/ QUESTIONS

_____
_____
_____
_____
_____
_____
_____
_____
_____
_____
_____
_____
_____
_____
_____
_____
_____
_____
_____

TODAY'S MAJIC
Learn a latin syllabus figure today.

PLANNING PRACTICE

DATE: _____

DAYS UNTIL NATIONALS: _____

TIME	WHAT	FOCUS	TYPE	SUCCESS

DAILY NOTES/ QUESTIONS

_____
_____
_____
_____
_____
_____
_____
_____
_____
_____
_____
_____
_____
_____
_____
_____
_____
_____

TODAY'S MAJIC
Why do you dance today?

PLANNING PRACTICE

DATE: _____

DAYS UNTIL NATIONALS: _____

TIME	WHAT	FOCUS	TYPE	SUCCESS

DAILY NOTES/ QUESTIONS

_____
_____
_____
_____
_____
_____
_____
_____
_____
_____
_____
_____
_____
_____
_____
_____
_____

TODAY'S MAJIC

Learn a rhythm syllabus figure today.

PLANNING PRACTICE

DATE: _____

DAYS UNTIL NATIONALS: _____

TIME	WHAT	FOCUS	TYPE	SUCCESS

DAILY NOTES/ QUESTIONS

_____
_____
_____
_____
_____
_____
_____
_____
_____
_____
_____
_____
_____
_____
_____
_____

TODAY'S MAJIC

What is one of your favorite memories from a comp?

PLANNING PRACTICE

DATE: _____

DAYS UNTIL NATIONALS: _____

TIME	WHAT	FOCUS	TYPE	SUCCESS

DAILY NOTES/ QUESTIONS

_____
_____
_____
_____
_____
_____
_____
_____
_____
_____
_____
_____
_____
_____
_____
_____
_____

TODAY'S MAJIC

What is your partner's favorite treat?

PLANNING PRACTICE

DATE: _____

DAYS UNTIL NATIONALS: _____

TIME	WHAT	FOCUS	TYPE	SUCCESS

DAILY NOTES/ QUESTIONS

_____
_____
_____
_____
_____
_____
_____
_____
_____
_____
_____
_____
_____
_____
_____
_____
_____
_____

TODAY'S MAJIC
Learn a smooth syllabus figure today.

PLANNING PRACTICE

DATE: _____

DAYS UNTIL NATIONALS: _____

TIME	WHAT	FOCUS	TYPE	SUCCESS

DAILY NOTES/ QUESTIONS

_____
_____
_____
_____
_____
_____
_____
_____
_____
_____
_____
_____
_____
_____
_____

TODAY'S MAJIC

What's your favorite dance today?

PLANNING PRACTICE
DATE: _____
DAYS UNTIL NATIONALS: _____

TIME	WHAT	FOCUS	TYPE	SUCCESS

DAILY NOTES/ QUESTIONS

_____
_____
_____
_____
_____
_____
_____
_____
_____
_____
_____
_____
_____
_____
_____
_____

TODAY'S MAJIC
Learn a latin syllabus figure today.

PLANNING PRACTICE

DATE: _____

DAYS UNTIL NATIONALS: _____

TIME	WHAT	FOCUS	TYPE	SUCCESS

DAILY NOTES/ QUESTIONS

_____
_____
_____
_____
_____
_____
_____
_____
_____
_____
_____
_____
_____
_____
_____
_____
_____
_____

TODAY'S MAJIC
What do love about your partner?

PLANNING PRACTICE

DATE: _____

DAYS UNTIL NATIONALS: _____

TIME	WHAT	FOCUS	TYPE	SUCCESS

DAILY NOTES/ QUESTIONS

_____
_____
_____
_____
_____
_____
_____
_____
_____
_____
_____
_____
_____
_____
_____
_____
_____

TODAY'S MAJIC
Learn a standard syllabus figure today.

PLANNING PRACTICE

DATE: _____

DAYS UNTIL NATIONALS: _____

TIME	WHAT	FOCUS	TYPE	SUCCESS

DAILY NOTES/ QUESTIONS

_____
_____
_____
_____
_____
_____
_____
_____
_____
_____
_____
_____
_____
_____
_____
_____
_____

TODAY'S MAJIC

What's your partner's favorite dance today?

PLANNING PRACTICE

DATE: _____

DAYS UNTIL NATIONALS: _____

TIME	WHAT	FOCUS	TYPE	SUCCESS

DAILY NOTES/ QUESTIONS

_____
_____
_____
_____
_____
_____
_____
_____
_____
_____
_____
_____
_____
_____
_____
_____
_____

TODAY'S MAJIC
What funny thing happened recently in practice?

PLANNING PRACTICE

DATE: _____

DAYS UNTIL NATIONALS: _____

TIME	WHAT	FOCUS	TYPE	SUCCESS

DAILY NOTES/ QUESTIONS

_____
_____
_____
_____
_____
_____
_____
_____
_____
_____
_____
_____
_____
_____
_____
_____
_____
_____

TODAY'S MAJIC

Learn a smooth syllabus figure today.

PLANNING PRACTICE

DATE: _____

DAYS UNTIL NATIONALS: _____

TIME	WHAT	FOCUS	TYPE	SUCCESS

DAILY NOTES/ QUESTIONS

_____
_____
_____
_____
_____
_____
_____
_____
_____
_____
_____
_____
_____
_____
_____
_____
_____

TODAY'S MAJIC
What do you appreciate
about your partner?

PLANNING PRACTICE

DATE: _____

DAYS UNTIL NATIONALS: _____

TIME	WHAT	FOCUS	TYPE	SUCCESS

DAILY NOTES/ QUESTIONS

_____
_____
_____
_____
_____
_____
_____
_____
_____
_____
_____
_____
_____
_____
_____
_____
_____

TODAY'S MAJIC
Why do you dance today?

PLANNING PRACTICE

DATE: _____

DAYS UNTIL NATIONALS: _____

TIME	WHAT	FOCUS	TYPE	SUCCESS

DAILY NOTES/ QUESTIONS

_____
_____
_____
_____
_____
_____
_____
_____
_____
_____
_____
_____
_____
_____
_____
_____
_____

TODAY'S MAJIC
Learn a rhythm syllabus
figure today.

PLANNING PRACTICE

DATE: _____

DAYS UNTIL NATIONALS: _____

TIME	WHAT	FOCUS	TYPE	SUCCESS

DAILY NOTES/ QUESTIONS

_____
_____
_____
_____
_____
_____
_____
_____
_____
_____
_____
_____
_____
_____
_____
_____
_____
_____
_____

TODAY'S MAJIC
Learn a latin syllabus figure today.

PLANNING PRACTICE

DATE: _____

DAYS UNTIL NATIONALS: _____

TIME	WHAT	FOCUS	TYPE	SUCCESS

DAILY NOTES/ QUESTIONS

_____
_____
_____
_____
_____
_____
_____
_____
_____
_____
_____
_____
_____
_____
_____
_____

TODAY'S MAJIC
What's your favorite dance today?

PLANNING PRACTICE

DATE: _____

DAYS UNTIL NATIONALS: _____

TIME	WHAT	FOCUS	TYPE	SUCCESS

DAILY NOTES/ QUESTIONS

_____
_____
_____
_____
_____
_____
_____
_____
_____
_____
_____
_____
_____
_____
_____
_____
_____

TODAY'S MAJIC
What do love about your partner?

PLANNING PRACTICE

DATE: _____

DAYS UNTIL NATIONALS: _____

TIME	WHAT	FOCUS	TYPE	SUCCESS

DAILY NOTES/ QUESTIONS

_____
_____
_____
_____
_____
_____
_____
_____
_____
_____
_____
_____
_____
_____
_____
_____

TODAY'S MAJIC

Learn a standard syllabus figure today.

PLANNING PRACTICE

DATE: _____

DAYS UNTIL NATIONALS: _____

TIME	WHAT	FOCUS	TYPE	SUCCESS

DAILY NOTES/ QUESTIONS

_____
_____
_____
_____
_____
_____
_____
_____
_____
_____
_____
_____
_____
_____
_____
_____
_____

TODAY'S MAJIC
Dance to your favorite song today.

PLANNING PRACTICE

DATE: _____

DAYS UNTIL NATIONALS: _____

TIME	WHAT	FOCUS	TYPE	SUCCESS

DAILY NOTES/ QUESTIONS

_____
_____
_____
_____
_____
_____
_____
_____
_____
_____
_____
_____
_____
_____
_____
_____
_____
_____

TODAY'S MAJIC
Learn a smooth syllabus figure today.

PLANNING PRACTICE

DATE: _____

DAYS UNTIL NATIONALS: _____

TIME	WHAT	FOCUS	TYPE	SUCCESS

DAILY NOTES/ QUESTIONS

_____
_____
_____
_____
_____
_____
_____
_____
_____
_____
_____
_____
_____
_____
_____
_____

TODAY'S MAJIC

What funny thing happened recently in practice?

PLANNING PRACTICE

DATE: _____

DAYS UNTIL NATIONALS: _____

TIME	WHAT	FOCUS	TYPE	SUCCESS

DAILY NOTES/ QUESTIONS

_____
_____
_____
_____
_____
_____
_____
_____
_____
_____
_____
_____
_____
_____
_____
_____
_____

TODAY'S MAJIC
Learn a rhythm syllabus figure today.

PLANNING PRACTICE

DATE: _____

DAYS UNTIL NATIONALS: _____

TIME	WHAT	FOCUS	TYPE	SUCCESS

DAILY NOTES/ QUESTIONS

_____
_____
_____
_____
_____
_____
_____
_____
_____
_____
_____
_____
_____
_____
_____
_____
_____
_____

TODAY'S MAJIC
What one thing do you want to improve in your dancing today?

PLANNING PRACTICE

DATE: _____

DAYS UNTIL NATIONALS: _____

TIME	WHAT	FOCUS	TYPE	SUCCESS

DAILY NOTES/ QUESTIONS

_____
_____
_____
_____
_____
_____
_____
_____
_____
_____
_____
_____
_____
_____
_____
_____

TODAY'S MAJIC
What do you appreciate about your partner?

PLANNING PRACTICE

DATE: _____

DAYS UNTIL NATIONALS: _____

TIME	WHAT	FOCUS	TYPE	SUCCESS

DAILY NOTES/ QUESTIONS

_____
_____
_____
_____
_____
_____
_____
_____
_____
_____
_____
_____
_____
_____
_____
_____
_____

TODAY'S MAJIC
Learn a standard syllabus figure today.

PLANNING PRACTICE

DATE: _____

DAYS UNTIL NATIONALS: _____

TIME	WHAT	FOCUS	TYPE	SUCCESS

DAILY NOTES/ QUESTIONS

_____
_____
_____
_____
_____
_____
_____
_____
_____
_____
_____
_____
_____
_____
_____
_____
_____
_____

TODAY'S MAJIC

What's your partner's favorite dance today?

PLANNING PRACTICE

DATE: _____

DAYS UNTIL NATIONALS: _____

TIME	WHAT	FOCUS	TYPE	SUCCESS

DAILY NOTES/ QUESTIONS

_____
_____
_____
_____
_____
_____
_____
_____
_____
_____
_____
_____
_____
_____
_____
_____
_____

TODAY'S MAJIC

Learn a latin syllabus figure today.

PLANNING PRACTICE

DATE: _____

DAYS UNTIL NATIONALS: _____

TIME	WHAT	FOCUS	TYPE	SUCCESS

DAILY NOTES/ QUESTIONS

_____
_____
_____
_____
_____
_____
_____
_____
_____
_____
_____
_____
_____
_____
_____
_____
_____
_____

TODAY'S MAJIC
Why do you dance today?

PLANNING PRACTICE

DATE: _____

DAYS UNTIL NATIONALS: _____

TIME	WHAT	FOCUS	TYPE	SUCCESS

DAILY NOTES/ QUESTIONS

_____
_____
_____
_____
_____
_____
_____
_____
_____
_____
_____
_____
_____
_____
_____
_____
_____

TODAY'S MAJIC

Learn a rhythm syllabus figure today.

PLANNING PRACTICE

DATE: _____

DAYS UNTIL NATIONALS: _____

TIME	WHAT	FOCUS	TYPE	SUCCESS

DAILY NOTES/ QUESTIONS

_____
_____
_____
_____
_____
_____
_____
_____
_____
_____
_____
_____
_____
_____
_____
_____

TODAY'S MAJIC

What is one of your favorite memories from a comp?

PLANNING PRACTICE

DATE: _____

DAYS UNTIL NATIONALS: _____

TIME	WHAT	FOCUS	TYPE	SUCCESS

DAILY NOTES/ QUESTIONS

_____
_____
_____
_____
_____
_____
_____
_____
_____
_____
_____
_____
_____
_____
_____
_____
_____
_____

TODAY'S MAJIC
What is your partner's favorite drink?

PLANNING PRACTICE

DATE: _____

DAYS UNTIL NATIONALS: _____

TIME	WHAT	FOCUS	TYPE	SUCCESS

DAILY NOTES/ QUESTIONS

_____
_____
_____
_____
_____
_____
_____
_____
_____
_____
_____
_____
_____
_____
_____
_____
_____
_____

TODAY'S MAJIC

Learn a smooth syllabus figure today.

PLANNING PRACTICE

DATE: _____

DAYS UNTIL NATIONALS: _____

TIME	WHAT	FOCUS	TYPE	SUCCESS

DAILY NOTES/ QUESTIONS

_____
_____
_____
_____
_____
_____
_____
_____
_____
_____
_____
_____
_____
_____
_____
_____
_____

TODAY'S MAJIC

What's your favorite dance today?

PLANNING PRACTICE

DATE: _____

DAYS UNTIL NATIONALS: _____

TIME	WHAT	FOCUS	TYPE	SUCCESS

DAILY NOTES/ QUESTIONS

_____
_____
_____
_____
_____
_____
_____
_____
_____
_____
_____
_____
_____
_____
_____
_____
_____

TODAY'S MAJIC
Learn a latin syllabus figure today.

PLANNING PRACTICE

DATE: _____

DAYS UNTIL NATIONALS: _____

TIME	WHAT	FOCUS	TYPE	SUCCESS

DAILY NOTES/ QUESTIONS

_____
_____
_____
_____
_____
_____
_____
_____
_____
_____
_____
_____
_____
_____
_____
_____
_____
_____

TODAY'S MAJIC
What do love about your partner?

PLANNING PRACTICE

DATE: _____

DAYS UNTIL NATIONALS: _____

TIME	WHAT	FOCUS	TYPE	SUCCESS

DAILY NOTES/ QUESTIONS

_____
_____
_____
_____
_____
_____
_____
_____
_____
_____
_____
_____
_____
_____
_____
_____
_____
_____

TODAY'S MAJIC
Learn a standard syllabus figure today.

PLANNING PRACTICE

DATE: _____

DAYS UNTIL NATIONALS: _____

TIME	WHAT	FOCUS	TYPE	SUCCESS

DAILY NOTES/ QUESTIONS

_____
_____
_____
_____
_____
_____
_____
_____
_____
_____
_____
_____
_____
_____
_____
_____

TODAY'S MAJIC
What's your partner's favorite dance today?

PLANNING PRACTICE

DATE: _____

DAYS UNTIL NATIONALS: _____

TIME	WHAT	FOCUS	TYPE	SUCCESS

DAILY NOTES/ QUESTIONS

_____
_____
_____
_____
_____
_____
_____
_____
_____
_____
_____
_____
_____
_____
_____

TODAY'S MAJIC
What funny thing happened recently in practice?

PLANNING PRACTICE

DATE: _____

DAYS UNTIL NATIONALS: _____

TIME	WHAT	FOCUS	TYPE	SUCCESS

DAILY NOTES/ QUESTIONS

_____
_____
_____
_____
_____
_____
_____
_____
_____
_____
_____
_____
_____
_____
_____
_____
_____

TODAY'S MAJIC
Learn a smooth syllabus figure today.

PLANNING PRACTICE

DATE: _____

DAYS UNTIL NATIONALS: _____

TIME	WHAT	FOCUS	TYPE	SUCCESS

DAILY NOTES/ QUESTIONS

_____
_____
_____
_____
_____
_____
_____
_____
_____
_____
_____
_____
_____
_____
_____
_____
_____
_____

TODAY'S MAJIC
What do you appreciate about your partner?

PLANNING PRACTICE

DATE: _____

DAYS UNTIL NATIONALS: _____

TIME	WHAT	FOCUS	TYPE	SUCCESS

DAILY NOTES/ QUESTIONS

_____
_____
_____
_____
_____
_____
_____
_____
_____
_____
_____
_____
_____
_____
_____
_____

TODAY'S MAJIC
Why do you dance today?

PLANNING PRACTICE

DATE: _____

DAYS UNTIL NATIONALS: _____

TIME	WHAT	FOCUS	TYPE	SUCCESS

DAILY NOTES/ QUESTIONS

_____
_____
_____
_____
_____
_____
_____
_____
_____
_____
_____
_____
_____
_____
_____
_____
_____

TODAY'S MAJIC

Learn a rhythm syllabus figure today.

PLANNING PRACTICE

DATE: _____

DAYS UNTIL NATIONALS: _____

TIME	WHAT	FOCUS	TYPE	SUCCESS

DAILY NOTES/ QUESTIONS

_____
_____
_____
_____
_____
_____
_____
_____
_____
_____
_____
_____
_____
_____
_____
_____
_____
_____

TODAY'S MAJIC

Learn a latin syllabus figure today.

PLANNING PRACTICE

DATE: _____

DAYS UNTIL NATIONALS: _____

TIME	WHAT	FOCUS	TYPE	SUCCESS

DAILY NOTES/ QUESTIONS

_____
_____
_____
_____
_____
_____
_____
_____
_____
_____
_____
_____
_____
_____
_____
_____
_____

TODAY'S MAJIC
What's your favorite dance today?

PLANNING PRACTICE

DATE: _____

DAYS UNTIL NATIONALS: _____

TIME	WHAT	FOCUS	TYPE	SUCCESS

DAILY NOTES/ QUESTIONS

_____
_____
_____
_____
_____
_____
_____
_____
_____
_____
_____
_____
_____
_____
_____
_____

TODAY'S MAJIC

What do love about your partner?

PLANNING PRACTICE

DATE: _____

DAYS UNTIL NATIONALS: _____

TIME	WHAT	FOCUS	TYPE	SUCCESS

DAILY NOTES/ QUESTIONS

_____
_____
_____
_____
_____
_____
_____
_____
_____
_____
_____
_____
_____
_____
_____
_____

TODAY'S MAJIC
Learn a standard syllabus figure today.

PLANNING PRACTICE

DATE: _____

DAYS UNTIL NATIONALS: _____

TIME	WHAT	FOCUS	TYPE	SUCCESS

DAILY NOTES/ QUESTIONS

_____
_____
_____
_____
_____
_____
_____
_____
_____
_____
_____
_____
_____
_____
_____
_____
_____

TODAY'S MAJIC
Dance to your favorite song today.

PLANNING PRACTICE

DATE: _____

DAYS UNTIL NATIONALS: _____

TIME	WHAT	FOCUS	TYPE	SUCCESS

DAILY NOTES/ QUESTIONS

_____
_____
_____
_____
_____
_____
_____
_____
_____
_____
_____
_____
_____
_____
_____
_____

TODAY'S MAJIC

Learn a smooth syllabus figure today.

PLANNING PRACTICE

DATE: _____

DAYS UNTIL NATIONALS: _____

TIME	WHAT	FOCUS	TYPE	SUCCESS

DAILY NOTES/ QUESTIONS

_____
_____
_____
_____
_____
_____
_____
_____
_____
_____
_____
_____
_____
_____
_____
_____
_____

TODAY'S MAJIC
What funny thing happened recently in practice?

PLANNING PRACTICE

DATE: _____

DAYS UNTIL NATIONALS: _____

TIME	WHAT	FOCUS	TYPE	SUCCESS

DAILY NOTES/ QUESTIONS

_____
_____
_____
_____
_____
_____
_____
_____
_____
_____
_____
_____
_____
_____
_____
_____
_____

TODAY'S MAJIC

Learn a rhythm syllabus figure today.

PLANNING PRACTICE

DATE: _____

DAYS UNTIL NATIONALS: _____

TIME	WHAT	FOCUS	TYPE	SUCCESS

DAILY NOTES/ QUESTIONS

_____
_____
_____
_____
_____
_____
_____
_____
_____
_____
_____
_____
_____
_____
_____
_____

TODAY'S MAJIC

What one thing do you want to improve in your dancing today?

PLANNING PRACTICE

DATE: _____

DAYS UNTIL NATIONALS: _____

TIME	WHAT	FOCUS	TYPE	SUCCESS

DAILY NOTES/ QUESTIONS

_____
_____
_____
_____
_____
_____
_____
_____
_____
_____
_____
_____
_____
_____
_____
_____
_____
_____

TODAY'S MAJIC
What do you appreciate about your partner?

PLANNING PRACTICE

DATE: _____

DAYS UNTIL NATIONALS: _____

TIME	WHAT	FOCUS	TYPE	SUCCESS

DAILY NOTES/ QUESTIONS

_____

_____

_____

_____

_____

_____

_____

_____

_____

_____

_____

_____

_____

_____

_____

_____

TODAY'S MAJIC

Learn a standard syllabus figure today.

PLANNING PRACTICE

DATE: _____

DAYS UNTIL NATIONALS: _____

TIME	WHAT	FOCUS	TYPE	SUCCESS

DAILY NOTES/ QUESTIONS

_____
_____
_____
_____
_____
_____
_____
_____
_____
_____
_____
_____
_____
_____
_____
_____

TODAY'S MAJIC
What's your partner's favorite dance today?

PLANNING PRACTICE

DATE: _____

DAYS UNTIL NATIONALS: _____

TIME	WHAT	FOCUS	TYPE	SUCCESS

DAILY NOTES/ QUESTIONS

_____
_____
_____
_____
_____
_____
_____
_____
_____
_____
_____
_____
_____
_____
_____
_____
_____

TODAY'S MAJIC
Learn a latin syllabus figure today.

PLANNING PRACTICE

DATE: _____

DAYS UNTIL NATIONALS: _____

TIME	WHAT	FOCUS	TYPE	SUCCESS

DAILY NOTES/ QUESTIONS

_____
_____
_____
_____
_____
_____
_____
_____
_____
_____
_____
_____
_____
_____
_____
_____
_____
_____

TODAY'S MAJIC
Why do you dance today?

PLANNING PRACTICE

DATE: _____

DAYS UNTIL NATIONALS: _____

TIME	WHAT	FOCUS	TYPE	SUCCESS

DAILY NOTES/ QUESTIONS

_____
_____
_____
_____
_____
_____
_____
_____
_____
_____
_____
_____
_____
_____
_____
_____

TODAY'S MAJIC

Learn a rhythm syllabus figure today.

PLANNING PRACTICE

DATE: _____

DAYS UNTIL NATIONALS: _____

TIME	WHAT	FOCUS	TYPE	SUCCESS

DAILY NOTES/ QUESTIONS

_____
_____
_____
_____
_____
_____
_____
_____
_____
_____
_____
_____
_____
_____
_____

TODAY'S MAJIC
What is one of your favorite memories from a comp?

PLANNING PRACTICE

DATE: _____

DAYS UNTIL NATIONALS: _____

TIME	WHAT	FOCUS	TYPE	SUCCESS

DAILY NOTES/ QUESTIONS

_____
_____
_____
_____
_____
_____
_____
_____
_____
_____
_____
_____
_____
_____
_____
_____
_____
_____

TODAY'S MAJIC

What is your partner's favorite ice cream?

PLANNING PRACTICE

DATE: _____

DAYS UNTIL NATIONALS: _____

TIME	WHAT	FOCUS	TYPE	SUCCESS

DAILY NOTES/ QUESTIONS

_____
_____
_____
_____
_____
_____
_____
_____
_____
_____
_____
_____
_____
_____
_____
_____

TODAY'S MAJIC
Learn a smooth syllabus figure today.

PLANNING PRACTICE

DATE: _____

DAYS UNTIL NATIONALS: _____

TIME	WHAT	FOCUS	TYPE	SUCCESS

DAILY NOTES/ QUESTIONS

_____
_____
_____
_____
_____
_____
_____
_____
_____
_____
_____
_____
_____
_____
_____
_____

TODAY'S MAJIC

What's your favorite dance today?

PLANNING PRACTICE

DATE: _____

DAYS UNTIL NATIONALS: _____

TIME	WHAT	FOCUS	TYPE	SUCCESS

DAILY NOTES/ QUESTIONS

_____
_____
_____
_____
_____
_____
_____
_____
_____
_____
_____
_____
_____
_____
_____
_____

TODAY'S MAJIC
Learn a latin syllabus figure today.

PLANNING PRACTICE

DATE: _____

DAYS UNTIL NATIONALS: _____

TIME	WHAT	FOCUS	TYPE	SUCCESS

DAILY NOTES/ QUESTIONS

_____
_____
_____
_____
_____
_____
_____
_____
_____
_____
_____
_____
_____
_____
_____
_____
_____

TODAY'S MAJIC

What do love about your partner?

PLANNING PRACTICE

DATE: _____

DAYS UNTIL NATIONALS: _____

TIME	WHAT	FOCUS	TYPE	SUCCESS

DAILY NOTES/ QUESTIONS

_____
_____
_____
_____
_____
_____
_____
_____
_____
_____
_____
_____
_____
_____
_____
_____
_____
_____

TODAY'S MAJIC
Learn a standard syllabus figure today.

PLANNING PRACTICE

DATE: _____

DAYS UNTIL NATIONALS: _____

TIME	WHAT	FOCUS	TYPE	SUCCESS

DAILY NOTES/ QUESTIONS

_____
_____
_____
_____
_____
_____
_____
_____
_____
_____
_____
_____
_____
_____
_____

TODAY'S MAJIC

What's your partner's favorite dance today?

PLANNING PRACTICE

DATE: _____

DAYS UNTIL NATIONALS: _____

TIME	WHAT	FOCUS	TYPE	SUCCESS

DAILY NOTES/ QUESTIONS

_____
_____
_____
_____
_____
_____
_____
_____
_____
_____
_____
_____
_____
_____
_____
_____
_____

TODAY'S MAJIC
What funny thing happened recently in practice?

PLANNING PRACTICE

DATE: _____

DAYS UNTIL NATIONALS: _____

TIME	WHAT	FOCUS	TYPE	SUCCESS

DAILY NOTES/ QUESTIONS

_____
_____
_____
_____
_____
_____
_____
_____
_____
_____
_____
_____
_____
_____
_____
_____
_____
_____

TODAY'S MAJIC
Learn a smooth syllabus figure today.

PLANNING PRACTICE

DATE: _____

DAYS UNTIL NATIONALS: _____

TIME	WHAT	FOCUS	TYPE	SUCCESS

DAILY NOTES/ QUESTIONS

_____
_____
_____
_____
_____
_____
_____
_____
_____
_____
_____
_____
_____
_____
_____
_____

TODAY'S MAJIC
What do you appreciate
about your partner?

PLANNING PRACTICE

DATE: _____

DAYS UNTIL NATIONALS: _____

TIME	WHAT	FOCUS	TYPE	SUCCESS

DAILY NOTES/ QUESTIONS

_____
_____
_____
_____
_____
_____
_____
_____
_____
_____
_____
_____
_____
_____
_____
_____

TODAY'S MAJIC
Why do you dance today?

PLANNING PRACTICE

DATE: _____

DAYS UNTIL NATIONALS: _____

TIME	WHAT	FOCUS	TYPE	SUCCESS

DAILY NOTES/ QUESTIONS

_____
_____
_____
_____
_____
_____
_____
_____
_____
_____
_____
_____
_____
_____
_____
_____
_____

TODAY'S MAJIC
Learn a rhythm syllabus figure today.

PLANNING PRACTICE

DATE: _____

DAYS UNTIL NATIONALS: _____

TIME	WHAT	FOCUS	TYPE	SUCCESS

DAILY NOTES/ QUESTIONS

_____
_____
_____
_____
_____
_____
_____
_____
_____
_____
_____
_____
_____
_____
_____
_____
_____

TODAY'S MAJIC
Learn a latin syllabus figure today.

PLANNING PRACTICE

DATE: _____

DAYS UNTIL NATIONALS: _____

TIME	WHAT	FOCUS	TYPE	SUCCESS

DAILY NOTES/ QUESTIONS

_____
_____
_____
_____
_____
_____
_____
_____
_____
_____
_____
_____
_____
_____
_____
_____
_____

TODAY'S MAJIC
What's your favorite
dance today?

PLANNING PRACTICE

DATE: _____

DAYS UNTIL NATIONALS: _____

TIME	WHAT	FOCUS	TYPE	SUCCESS

DAILY NOTES/ QUESTIONS

_____
_____
_____
_____
_____
_____
_____
_____
_____
_____
_____
_____
_____
_____
_____
_____

TODAY'S MAJIC

What do love about your partner?

PLANNING PRACTICE

DATE: _____

DAYS UNTIL NATIONALS: _____

TIME	WHAT	FOCUS	TYPE	SUCCESS

DAILY NOTES/ QUESTIONS

_____
_____
_____
_____
_____
_____
_____
_____
_____
_____
_____
_____
_____
_____
_____

TODAY'S MAJIC

Learn a standard syllabus figure today.

PLANNING PRACTICE

DATE: _____

DAYS UNTIL NATIONALS: _____

TIME	WHAT	FOCUS	TYPE	SUCCESS

DAILY NOTES/ QUESTIONS

_____
_____
_____
_____
_____
_____
_____
_____
_____
_____
_____
_____
_____
_____
_____
_____

TODAY'S MAJIC
Dance to your favorite song today.

PLANNING PRACTICE

DATE: _____

DAYS UNTIL NATIONALS: _____

TIME	WHAT	FOCUS	TYPE	SUCCESS

DAILY NOTES/ QUESTIONS

_____
_____
_____
_____
_____
_____
_____
_____
_____
_____
_____
_____
_____
_____
_____
_____
_____

TODAY'S MAJIC

Learn a smooth syllabus figure today.

PLANNING PRACTICE

DATE: _____

DAYS UNTIL NATIONALS: _____

TIME	WHAT	FOCUS	TYPE	SUCCESS

DAILY NOTES/ QUESTIONS

_____
_____
_____
_____
_____
_____
_____
_____
_____
_____
_____
_____
_____
_____
_____
_____
_____

TODAY'S MAJIC
What funny thing happened recently in practice?

PLANNING PRACTICE

DATE: _____

DAYS UNTIL NATIONALS: _____

TIME	WHAT	FOCUS	TYPE	SUCCESS

DAILY NOTES/ QUESTIONS

_____
_____
_____
_____
_____
_____
_____
_____
_____
_____
_____
_____
_____
_____
_____
_____
_____

TODAY'S MAJIC

Learn a rhythm syllabus figure today.

PLANNING PRACTICE
DATE: _____

DAYS UNTIL NATIONALS: _____

TIME	WHAT	FOCUS	TYPE	SUCCESS

DAILY NOTES/ QUESTIONS

_____
_____
_____
_____
_____
_____
_____
_____
_____
_____
_____
_____
_____
_____
_____
_____

TODAY'S MAJIC
What one thing do you want to improve in your dancing today?

PLANNING PRACTICE

DATE: _____

DAYS UNTIL NATIONALS: _____

TIME	WHAT	FOCUS	TYPE	SUCCESS

DAILY NOTES/ QUESTIONS

_____
_____
_____
_____
_____
_____
_____
_____
_____
_____
_____
_____
_____
_____
_____
_____
_____
_____

TODAY'S MAJIC
What do you appreciate about your partner?

PLANNING PRACTICE

DATE: _____

DAYS UNTIL NATIONALS: _____

TIME	WHAT	FOCUS	TYPE	SUCCESS

DAILY NOTES/ QUESTIONS

_____
_____
_____
_____
_____
_____
_____
_____
_____
_____
_____
_____
_____
_____
_____
_____

TODAY'S MAJIC
Learn a standard syllabus figure today.

PLANNING PRACTICE

DATE: _____

DAYS UNTIL NATIONALS: _____

TIME	WHAT	FOCUS	TYPE	SUCCESS

DAILY NOTES/ QUESTIONS

_____
_____
_____
_____
_____
_____
_____
_____
_____
_____
_____
_____
_____
_____
_____
_____

TODAY'S MAJIC
What's your partner's favorite dance today?

PLANNING PRACTICE

DATE: _____

DAYS UNTIL NATIONALS: _____

TIME	WHAT	FOCUS	TYPE	SUCCESS

DAILY NOTES/ QUESTIONS

_____
_____
_____
_____
_____
_____
_____
_____
_____
_____
_____
_____
_____
_____
_____
_____

TODAY'S MAJIC
Learn a latin syllabus figure today.

PLANNING PRACTICE

DATE: _____

DAYS UNTIL NATIONALS: _____

TIME	WHAT	FOCUS	TYPE	SUCCESS

DAILY NOTES/ QUESTIONS

_____
_____
_____
_____
_____
_____
_____
_____
_____
_____
_____
_____
_____
_____
_____
_____
_____

TODAY'S MAJIC
Why do you dance today?

PLANNING PRACTICE

DATE: _____

DAYS UNTIL NATIONALS: _____

TIME	WHAT	FOCUS	TYPE	SUCCESS

DAILY NOTES/ QUESTIONS

_____
_____
_____
_____
_____
_____
_____
_____
_____
_____
_____
_____
_____
_____
_____

TODAY'S MAJIC
Learn a rhythm syllabus figure today.

PLANNING PRACTICE

DATE: _____

DAYS UNTIL NATIONALS: _____

TIME	WHAT	FOCUS	TYPE	SUCCESS

DAILY NOTES/ QUESTIONS

_____
_____
_____
_____
_____
_____
_____
_____
_____
_____
_____
_____
_____
_____
_____
_____

TODAY'S MAJIC
What is one of your favorite memories from a comp?

PLANNING PRACTICE

DATE: _____

DAYS UNTIL NATIONALS: _____

TIME	WHAT	FOCUS	TYPE	SUCCESS

DAILY NOTES/ QUESTIONS

_____
_____
_____
_____
_____
_____
_____
_____
_____
_____
_____
_____
_____
_____
_____
_____
_____

TODAY'S MAJIC

What is your partner's favorite restaurant?

PLANNING PRACTICE

DATE: _____

DAYS UNTIL NATIONALS: _____

TIME	WHAT	FOCUS	TYPE	SUCCESS

DAILY NOTES/ QUESTIONS

_____
_____
_____
_____
_____
_____
_____
_____
_____
_____
_____
_____
_____
_____
_____
_____
_____

TODAY'S MAJIC
Learn a smooth syllabus figure today.

PLANNING PRACTICE

DATE: _____

DAYS UNTIL NATIONALS: _____

TIME	WHAT	FOCUS	TYPE	SUCCESS

DAILY NOTES/ QUESTIONS

_____
_____
_____
_____
_____
_____
_____
_____
_____
_____
_____
_____
_____
_____
_____
_____
_____

TODAY'S MAJIC

What's your favorite dance today?

PLANNING PRACTICE

DATE: _____

DAYS UNTIL NATIONALS: _____

TIME	WHAT	FOCUS	TYPE	SUCCESS

DAILY NOTES/ QUESTIONS

_____
_____
_____
_____
_____
_____
_____
_____
_____
_____
_____
_____
_____
_____
_____
_____
_____

TODAY'S MAJIC
Learn a latin syllabus figure today.

PLANNING PRACTICE

DATE: _____

DAYS UNTIL NATIONALS: _____

TIME	WHAT	FOCUS	TYPE	SUCCESS

DAILY NOTES/ QUESTIONS

_____
_____
_____
_____
_____
_____
_____
_____
_____
_____
_____
_____
_____
_____
_____
_____
_____
_____
_____

TODAY'S MAJIC

What do love about your partner?

PLANNING PRACTICE

DATE: _____

DAYS UNTIL NATIONALS: _____

TIME	WHAT	FOCUS	TYPE	SUCCESS

DAILY NOTES/ QUESTIONS

_____
_____
_____
_____
_____
_____
_____
_____
_____
_____
_____
_____
_____
_____
_____
_____
_____
_____

TODAY'S MAJIC

Learn a standard syllabus figure today.

PLANNING PRACTICE

DATE: _____

DAYS UNTIL NATIONALS: _____

TIME	WHAT	FOCUS	TYPE	SUCCESS

DAILY NOTES/ QUESTIONS

_____
_____
_____
_____
_____
_____
_____
_____
_____
_____
_____
_____
_____
_____
_____
_____

TODAY'S MAJIC

What's your partner's favorite dance today?

PLANNING PRACTICE

DATE: _____

DAYS UNTIL NATIONALS: _____

TIME	WHAT	FOCUS	TYPE	SUCCESS

DAILY NOTES/ QUESTIONS

_____
_____
_____
_____
_____
_____
_____
_____
_____
_____
_____
_____
_____
_____
_____
_____

TODAY'S MAJIC
What funny thing happened recently in practice?

PLANNING PRACTICE

DATE: _____

DAYS UNTIL NATIONALS: _____

TIME	WHAT	FOCUS	TYPE	SUCCESS

DAILY NOTES/ QUESTIONS

_____
_____
_____
_____
_____
_____
_____
_____
_____
_____
_____
_____
_____
_____
_____
_____
_____
_____
_____

TODAY'S MAJIC

Learn a smooth syllabus figure today.

PLANNING PRACTICE

DATE: _____

DAYS UNTIL NATIONALS: _____

TIME	WHAT	FOCUS	TYPE	SUCCESS

DAILY NOTES/ QUESTIONS

_____
_____
_____
_____
_____
_____
_____
_____
_____
_____
_____
_____
_____
_____
_____
_____
_____
_____

TODAY'S MAJIC
What do you appreciate
about your partner?

PLANNING PRACTICE

DATE: _____

DAYS UNTIL NATIONALS: _____

TIME	WHAT	FOCUS	TYPE	SUCCESS

DAILY NOTES/ QUESTIONS

_____
_____
_____
_____
_____
_____
_____
_____
_____
_____
_____
_____
_____
_____
_____
_____
_____

TODAY'S MAJIC
Why do you dance today?

PLANNING PRACTICE

DATE: _____

DAYS UNTIL NATIONALS: _____

TIME	WHAT	FOCUS	TYPE	SUCCESS

DAILY NOTES/ QUESTIONS

_____
_____
_____
_____
_____
_____
_____
_____
_____
_____
_____
_____
_____
_____
_____
_____

TODAY'S MAJIC
Learn a rhythm syllabus figure today.

PLANNING PRACTICE

DATE: _____

DAYS UNTIL NATIONALS: _____

TIME	WHAT	FOCUS	TYPE	SUCCESS

DAILY NOTES/ QUESTIONS

_____
_____
_____
_____
_____
_____
_____
_____
_____
_____
_____
_____
_____
_____
_____
_____
_____
_____

TODAY'S MAJIC
Learn a latin syllabus figure today.

PLANNING PRACTICE

DATE: _____

DAYS UNTIL NATIONALS: _____

TIME	WHAT	FOCUS	TYPE	SUCCESS

DAILY NOTES/ QUESTIONS

_____
_____
_____
_____
_____
_____
_____
_____
_____
_____
_____
_____
_____
_____
_____
_____
_____
_____
_____

TODAY'S MAJIC
What's your favorite
dance today?

PLANNING PRACTICE

DATE: _____

DAYS UNTIL NATIONALS: _____

TIME	WHAT	FOCUS	TYPE	SUCCESS

DAILY NOTES/ QUESTIONS

_____
_____
_____
_____
_____
_____
_____
_____
_____
_____
_____
_____
_____
_____
_____
_____

TODAY'S MAJIC
What do love about your partner?

PLANNING PRACTICE

DATE: _____

DAYS UNTIL NATIONALS: _____

TIME	WHAT	FOCUS	TYPE	SUCCESS

DAILY NOTES/ QUESTIONS

_____
_____
_____
_____
_____
_____
_____
_____
_____
_____
_____
_____
_____
_____
_____
_____
_____

TODAY'S MAJIC
Learn a standard syllabus figure today.

PLANNING PRACTICE

DATE: _____

DAYS UNTIL NATIONALS: _____

TIME	WHAT	FOCUS	TYPE	SUCCESS

DAILY NOTES/ QUESTIONS

_____
_____
_____
_____
_____
_____
_____
_____
_____
_____
_____
_____
_____
_____
_____
_____
_____
_____

TODAY'S MAJIC
Dance to your favorite song today.

PLANNING PRACTICE

DATE: _____

DAYS UNTIL NATIONALS: _____

TIME	WHAT	FOCUS	TYPE	SUCCESS

DAILY NOTES/ QUESTIONS

_____
_____
_____
_____
_____
_____
_____
_____
_____
_____
_____
_____
_____
_____
_____
_____
_____
_____

TODAY'S MAJIC

Learn a smooth syllabus
figure today.

PLANNING PRACTICE

DATE: _____

DAYS UNTIL NATIONALS: _____

TIME	WHAT	FOCUS	TYPE	SUCCESS

DAILY NOTES/ QUESTIONS

_____
_____
_____
_____
_____
_____
_____
_____
_____
_____
_____
_____
_____
_____
_____

TODAY'S MAJIC
What funny thing happened recently in practice?

PLANNING PRACTICE

DATE: _____

DAYS UNTIL NATIONALS: _____

TIME	WHAT	FOCUS	TYPE	SUCCESS

DAILY NOTES/ QUESTIONS

_____
_____
_____
_____
_____
_____
_____
_____
_____
_____
_____
_____
_____
_____
_____

TODAY'S MAJIC
Learn a rhythm syllabus figure today.

PLANNING PRACTICE

DATE: _____

DAYS UNTIL NATIONALS: _____

TIME	WHAT	FOCUS	TYPE	SUCCESS

DAILY NOTES/ QUESTIONS

_____
_____
_____
_____
_____
_____
_____
_____
_____
_____
_____
_____
_____
_____
_____
_____
_____

TODAY'S MAJIC

What one thing do you want to improve in your dancing today?

PLANNING PRACTICE

DATE: _____

DAYS UNTIL NATIONALS: _____

TIME	WHAT	FOCUS	TYPE	SUCCESS

DAILY NOTES/ QUESTIONS

_____
_____
_____
_____
_____
_____
_____
_____
_____
_____
_____
_____
_____
_____
_____
_____
_____

TODAY'S MAJIC

What do you appreciate about your partner?

PLANNING PRACTICE

DATE: _____

DAYS UNTIL NATIONALS: _____

TIME	WHAT	FOCUS	TYPE	SUCCESS

DAILY NOTES/ QUESTIONS

_____
_____
_____
_____
_____
_____
_____
_____
_____
_____
_____
_____
_____
_____
_____
_____

TODAY'S MAJIC

Learn a standard syllabus figure today.

PLANNING PRACTICE

DATE: _____

DAYS UNTIL NATIONALS: _____

TIME	WHAT	FOCUS	TYPE	SUCCESS

DAILY NOTES/ QUESTIONS

_____
_____
_____
_____
_____
_____
_____
_____
_____
_____
_____
_____
_____
_____
_____
_____

TODAY'S MAJIC
What's your partner's favorite dance today?

PLANNING PRACTICE

DATE: _____

DAYS UNTIL NATIONALS: _____

TIME	WHAT	FOCUS	TYPE	SUCCESS

DAILY NOTES/ QUESTIONS

_____
_____
_____
_____
_____
_____
_____
_____
_____
_____
_____
_____
_____
_____
_____
_____
_____
_____
_____

TODAY'S MAJIC

Learn a latin syllabus figure today.

PLANNING PRACTICE

DATE: _____

DAYS UNTIL NATIONALS: _____

TIME	WHAT	FOCUS	TYPE	SUCCESS

DAILY NOTES/ QUESTIONS

_____
_____
_____
_____
_____
_____
_____
_____
_____
_____
_____
_____
_____
_____
_____
_____
_____
_____

TODAY'S MAJIC
Why do you dance today?

PLANNING PRACTICE

DATE: _____

DAYS UNTIL NATIONALS: _____

TIME	WHAT	FOCUS	TYPE	SUCCESS

DAILY NOTES/ QUESTIONS

_____
_____
_____
_____
_____
_____
_____
_____
_____
_____
_____
_____
_____
_____
_____
_____
_____

TODAY'S MAJIC

Learn a rhythm syllabus figure today.

PLANNING PRACTICE

DATE: _____

DAYS UNTIL NATIONALS: _____

TIME	WHAT	FOCUS	TYPE	SUCCESS

DAILY NOTES/ QUESTIONS

_____
_____
_____
_____
_____
_____
_____
_____
_____
_____
_____
_____
_____
_____
_____
_____
_____

TODAY'S MAJIC

What is one of your favorite memories from a comp?

PLANNING PRACTICE

DATE: _____

DAYS UNTIL NATIONALS: _____

TIME	WHAT	FOCUS	TYPE	SUCCESS

DAILY NOTES/ QUESTIONS

_____
_____
_____
_____
_____
_____
_____
_____
_____
_____
_____
_____
_____
_____
_____
_____
_____
_____

TODAY'S MAJIC
What is your partner's favorite food?

PLANNING PRACTICE

DATE: _____

DAYS UNTIL NATIONALS: _____

TIME	WHAT	FOCUS	TYPE	SUCCESS

DAILY NOTES/ QUESTIONS

_____

_____

_____

_____

_____

_____

_____

_____

_____

_____

_____

_____

_____

_____

_____

_____

_____

_____

TODAY'S MAJIC
Learn a smooth syllabus
figure today.

PLANNING PRACTICE

DATE: _____

DAYS UNTIL NATIONALS: _____

TIME	WHAT	FOCUS	TYPE	SUCCESS

DAILY NOTES/ QUESTIONS

_____
_____
_____
_____
_____
_____
_____
_____
_____
_____
_____
_____
_____
_____
_____
_____
_____

TODAY'S MAJIC

What's your favorite dance today?

PLANNING PRACTICE

DATE: _____

DAYS UNTIL NATIONALS: _____

TIME	WHAT	FOCUS	TYPE	SUCCESS

DAILY NOTES/ QUESTIONS

_____
_____
_____
_____
_____
_____
_____
_____
_____
_____
_____
_____
_____
_____
_____
_____
_____

TODAY'S MAJIC
Learn a latin syllabus figure today.

PLANNING PRACTICE

DATE: _____

DAYS UNTIL NATIONALS: _____

TIME	WHAT	FOCUS	TYPE	SUCCESS

DAILY NOTES/ QUESTIONS

_____
_____
_____
_____
_____
_____
_____
_____
_____
_____
_____
_____
_____
_____
_____
_____
_____

TODAY'S MAJIC
What do love about your partner?

PLANNING PRACTICE

DATE: _____

DAYS UNTIL NATIONALS: _____

TIME	WHAT	FOCUS	TYPE	SUCCESS

DAILY NOTES/ QUESTIONS

_____
_____
_____
_____
_____
_____
_____
_____
_____
_____
_____
_____
_____
_____
_____
_____

TODAY'S MAJIC
Learn a standard syllabus figure today.

PLANNING PRACTICE

DATE: _____

DAYS UNTIL NATIONALS: _____

TIME	WHAT	FOCUS	TYPE	SUCCESS

DAILY NOTES/ QUESTIONS

_____
_____
_____
_____
_____
_____
_____
_____
_____
_____
_____
_____
_____
_____
_____
_____
_____
_____

TODAY'S MAJIC

What's your partner's favorite dance today?

PLANNING PRACTICE

DATE: _____

DAYS UNTIL NATIONALS: _____

TIME	WHAT	FOCUS	TYPE	SUCCESS

DAILY NOTES/ QUESTIONS

_____
_____
_____
_____
_____
_____
_____
_____
_____
_____
_____
_____
_____
_____
_____

TODAY'S MAJIC
What funny thing happened recently in practice?

PLANNING PRACTICE

DATE: _____

DAYS UNTIL NATIONALS: _____

TIME	WHAT	FOCUS	TYPE	SUCCESS

DAILY NOTES/ QUESTIONS

_____
_____
_____
_____
_____
_____
_____
_____
_____
_____
_____
_____
_____
_____
_____
_____
_____

TODAY'S MAJIC

Learn a smooth syllabus figure today.

PLANNING PRACTICE

DATE: _____

DAYS UNTIL NATIONALS: _____

TIME	WHAT	FOCUS	TYPE	SUCCESS

DAILY NOTES/ QUESTIONS

_____

_____

_____

_____

_____

_____

_____

_____

_____

_____

_____

_____

_____

_____

_____

_____

TODAY'S MAJIC
What do you appreciate about your partner?

PLANNING PRACTICE

DATE: _____

DAYS UNTIL NATIONALS: _____

TIME	WHAT	FOCUS	TYPE	SUCCESS

DAILY NOTES/ QUESTIONS

_____
_____
_____
_____
_____
_____
_____
_____
_____
_____
_____
_____
_____
_____
_____
_____

TODAY'S MAJIC
Why do you dance today?

PLANNING PRACTICE

DATE: _____

DAYS UNTIL NATIONALS: _____

TIME	WHAT	FOCUS	TYPE	SUCCESS

DAILY NOTES/ QUESTIONS

_____
_____
_____
_____
_____
_____
_____
_____
_____
_____
_____
_____
_____
_____
_____
_____

TODAY'S MAJIC
Learn a rhythm syllabus figure today.

PLANNING PRACTICE

DATE: _____

DAYS UNTIL NATIONALS: _____

TIME	WHAT	FOCUS	TYPE	SUCCESS

DAILY NOTES/ QUESTIONS

_____
_____
_____
_____
_____
_____
_____
_____
_____
_____
_____
_____
_____
_____
_____
_____
_____

TODAY'S MAJIC

Learn a latin syllabus figure today.

PLANNING PRACTICE

DATE: _____

DAYS UNTIL NATIONALS: _____

TIME	WHAT	FOCUS	TYPE	SUCCESS

DAILY NOTES/ QUESTIONS

_____
_____
_____
_____
_____
_____
_____
_____
_____
_____
_____
_____
_____
_____
_____
_____
_____
_____

TODAY'S MAJIC
What's your favorite
dance today?

PLANNING PRACTICE

DATE: _____

DAYS UNTIL NATIONALS: _____

TIME	WHAT	FOCUS	TYPE	SUCCESS

DAILY NOTES/ QUESTIONS

_____
_____
_____
_____
_____
_____
_____
_____
_____
_____
_____
_____
_____
_____
_____
_____
_____

TODAY'S MAJIC

What do love about your partner?

PLANNING PRACTICE

DATE: _____

DAYS UNTIL NATIONALS: _____

TIME	WHAT	FOCUS	TYPE	SUCCESS

DAILY NOTES/ QUESTIONS

_____
_____
_____
_____
_____
_____
_____
_____
_____
_____
_____
_____
_____
_____
_____
_____
_____

TODAY'S MAJIC
Learn a standard syllabus figure today.

Made in United States
North Haven, CT
18 November 2022

26925729R00148